Bankim Chandra Chatterji

The poison Tree

A Tale of Hindu Life in Bengal

Bankim Chandra Chatterji

The poison Tree
A Tale of Hindu Life in Bengal

ISBN/EAN: 9783743357242

Manufactured in Europe, USA, Canada, Australia, Japa

Cover: Foto ©ninafisch / pixelio.de

Manufactured and distributed by brebook publishing software (www.brebook.com)

Bankim Chandra Chatterji

The poison Tree

THE POISON TREE

A Tale of Hindu Life in Bengal

BY

BANKIM CHANDRA CHATTERJEE

TRANSLATED BY

MIRIAM S. KNIGHT

WITH A PREFACE BY

EDWIN ARNOLD, C.S.I.

London
T. FISHER UNWIN
26 PATERNOSTER SQUARE
1884

The Gresham Press:
UNWIN BROTHERS, CHILWORTH AND LONDON.

PREFACE

 HAD been asked by the accomplished lady who has translated the subjoined story to introduce it with a few words of comment to the English public. For that purpose I commenced the perusal of the proof sheets; but soon found that what was begun as a literary task became a real and singular pleasure, by reason of the author's vivid narrative, his skill in delineating character, and, beyond all, the striking and faithful pictures of Indian life with which his tale is filled. Nor do these qualities suffer, beyond what is always inevitable, in the transfer of the novel from its

original Bengali to English. Five years ago, Sir William Herschel, of the Bengal Civil Service, had the intention of translating this *Bisha Briksha;* but surrendered the task, with the author's full consent, to Mrs. Knight, who has here performed it with very remarkable skill and success. To accomplish that, more was wanted than a competent knowledge of the language of the original and a fluent command of English : it was necessary to be familiar with the details of native life and manners, and to have a sufficient acquaintance with the religious, domestic, and social customs of Bengali homes. Possessing these, Mrs. Knight has now presented us with a modern Hindu novelette, smoothly readable throughout, perfectly well transferred from its vernacular (with such omissions as were necessary), and valuable, as I venture to affirm, to English readers as well from its skill in construction and intrinsic interest as for the light which it sheds upon the indoor existence of well-to-do Hindus, and the excellent specimen which it furnishes of the sort of indigenous literature happily growing popular in their cities and towns.

The author of "The Poison Tree" is Babu Bankim Chandra Chatterjee, a native gentleman of

Bengal, of superior intellectual acquisitions, who ranks unquestionably as the first living writer of fiction in his Presidency. His renown is widespread among native readers, who recognize the truthfulness and power of his descriptions, and are especially fond of "Krishna Kanta's Will," "Mrinalini," and this very story of the *Bisha Briksha*, which belongs to modern days in India, and to the new ideas which are spreading—not always quite happily—among the families of the land. Allowance being made for the loss which an original author cannot but sustain by the transfer of his style and method into another language and system of thought, it will be confessed, I think, that the reputation of "Bankim Babu" is well deserved, and that Bengal has here produced a writer of true genius, whose vivacious invention, dramatic force, and purity of aim, promise well for the new age of Indian vernacular literature.

It would be wrong to diminish the pleasure of the English reader by analysing the narrative and forestalling its plot. That which appears to me most striking and valuable in the book is the faithful view it gives of the gentleness and devotion of the average Hindu wife. Western people are wont to think that because marriages are arranged at an early age in India, and without the betrothed pair having the slightest share in the mutual choice, that wedded love of a sincere sort must be out of the question, and conjugal happiness very rare. The contrary is notably the case. Human nature is, somehow, so full of accidental harmonies, that a majority among the households thus constituted furnish examples of quiet felicity, established constancy, and, above all, of a devotedness on the part of the Hindu women to their husbands and children, which knows, so to speak, no limit. The self-sacrifice of Surja Mukhi in this tale would be next to impossible for any Western woman, but is positively common in the East, though our author so well displays the undoubted fact that feminine hearts are the same everywhere, and that custom cannot change the instincts of love. In Debendra the Babu paints successfully the "young Bengalee" of the present day, corrupted rather than elevated by his educational enlightenment. Nagendra is a good type of the ordinary well-to-do householder; Kunda Nandini, of the simple and graceful Hindu maiden; and Hira, of those passionate natures often concealed under the dark glances and regular features of the women of the Ganges Valley. In a word,

I am glad to recommend this translation to English readers, as a work which, apart from its charm in incident and narrative, will certainly give them just, if not complete, ideas of the ways of life of their fellow-subjects in Bengal.

EDWIN ARNOLD, C.S.I.

LONDON, *September* 10, 1884.

CONTENTS.

CHAPTER I.   AGE
NAGENDRA'S JOURNEY BY BOAT 1

CHAPTER II.
"COMING EVENTS CAST THEIR SHADOWS BEFORE" 13

CHAPTER III.
OF MANY SUBJECTS 23

CHAPTER IV.
TARA CHARAN 31

CHAPTER V.
OH! LOTUS-EYED, WHO ART THOU? 37

CHAPTER VI.
THE READER HAS CAUSE FOR GREAT DISPLEASURE 47

CHAPTER VII.
HARIDASI BOISNAVI 51

CHAPTER VIII.
THE BABU 63

CHAPTER IX.
SURJA MUKHI'S LETTER 73

CHAPTER X.
THE SPROUT 81

CHAPTER XI.
CAUGHT AT LAST 95

CHAPTER XII.
HIRA 101

CHAPTER XIII.
NO! 109

CHAPTER XIV.
LIKE TO LIKE 117

CHAPTER XV.
THE FORLORN ONE 127

CHAPTER XVI.
HIRA'S ENVY 137

CHAPTER XVII.
HIRA'S QUARREL. THE BUD OF THE POISON TREE 145

CHAPTER XVIII.
THE CAGED BIRD 155

CHAPTER XIX.
DESCENT 163

CONTENTS. xiii

CHAPTER XX.
GOOD NEWS 171

CHAPTER XXI.
SURJA MUKHI AND KAMAL MANI 183

CHAPTER XXII.
WHAT IS THE POISON TREE? 191

CHAPTER XXIII.
THE SEARCH 195

CHAPTER XXIV.
EVERY SORT OF HAPPINESS IS FLEETING ... 201

CHAPTER XXV.
THE FRUIT OF THE POISON TREE 205

CHAPTER XXVI.
THE SIGNS OF LOVE 213

CHAPTER XXVII.
BY THE ROADSIDE 221

CHAPTER XXVIII.
IS THERE HOPE? 227

CHAPTER XXIX.
HIRA'S POISON TREE HAS BLOSSOMED ... 235

CHAPTER XXX.
NEWS OF SURJA MUKHI 239

CHAPTER XXXI.
THOUGH ALL ELSE DIES, SUFFERING DIES NOT 249

CONTENTS.

CHAPTER XXXII.
THE FRUIT OF HIRA'S POISON TREE 259

CHAPTER XXXIII.
HIRA'S GRANDMOTHER 265

CHAPTER XXXIV.
A DARK HOUSE: A DARK LIFE 271

CHAPTER XXXV.
THE RETURN 277

CHAPTER XXXVI.
EXPLANATION 291

CHAPTER XXXVII.
THE SIMPLETON AND THE SERPENT 295

CHAPTER XXXVIII.
THE CATASTROPHE 303

CHAPTER XXXIX.
KUNDA'S TONGUE IS LOOSENED 307

CHAPTER XL.
THE END 311

GLOSSARY OF HINDU WORDS 315

For the assistance of the reader, the names of the principal characters in the tale are given—

NAGENDRA NATHA DATTA *A wealthy Zemindar.*
SURJA MUKHI . . . . . *His wife.*
DEBENDRA DATTA . . . *Cousin to Nagendra.*
SRISH CHANDRA MITTRA *Accountant in a Merchant's Office.*
KAMAL MANI . . . . . *His wife, sister to Nagendra.*
SATISH . . . . *Their baby boy.*
TARA CHARAN . . . . . *Adopted brother of Surja Mukhi.*
KUNDA NANDINI . . . *An Orphan Girl.*
HIRA . . . . *Servant in Nagendra's household.*

THE POISON TREE.

CHAPTER I.

NAGENDRA'S JOURNEY BY BOAT.

AGENDRA NATHA DATTA is about to travel by boat. It is the month *Joisto* (May—June), the time of storms. His wife, Surja Mukhi, had adjured him, saying, "Be careful; if a storm arises be sure you fasten the boat to the shore. Do not remain in the boat." Nagendra had consented to this, otherwise Surja Mukhi would not have permitted him to leave home; and unless he went to Calcutta his suits in the Courts would not prosper.

Nagendra Natha was a young man, about thirty years of age, a wealthy *zemindar* (landholder) in Zillah Govindpur. He dwelt in a small village which we shall call Haripur. He was travelling in his own boat. The first day or two passed without obstacle. The river flowed smoothly on— leaped, danced, cried out, restless, unending, playful. On shore, herdsmen were grazing their oxen —one sitting under a tree singing, another smoking, some fighting, others eating. Inland, husbandmen were driving the plough, beating the oxen, lavishing abuse upon them, in which the owner shared. The wives of the husbandmen, bearing vessels of water, some carrying a torn quilt, or a dirty mat, wearing a silver amulet round the neck, a ring in the nose, bracelets of brass on the arm, with unwashed garments, their skins blacker than ink, their hair unkempt, formed a chattering crowd. Among them one beauty was rubbing her head with mud, another beating a child, a third speaking with a neighbour in abuse of some nameless person, a fourth beating clothes on a plank. Further on, ladies from respectable villages adorned the *ghats* (landing-steps) with their appearance—the elders conversing, the middle-aged worshipping *Siva*, the younger covering their faces and plunging into the water; the boys and girls screaming, playing with mud, stealing the flowers offered in worship, swimming, throwing water over every one, sometimes stepping up to a lady, snatching away the image of *Siva* from her, and running off with it. The Brahmans, good tranquil men, recited the praises of *Ganga* (the sacred river Ganges) and performed their worship, sometimes, as they wiped their streaming hair, casting glances at the younger women.

In the sky, the white clouds float in the heated air. Below them fly the birds, like black dots. In the cocoa-nut trees, kites, like ministers of state, look around to see on what they can pounce; the cranes, being only small fry, stand raking in the mud; the *dahuk* (coloured herons), merry creatures, dive in the water; other birds of a lighter kind merely fly about. Market-boats sail along at good speed on their own behalf; ferry-boats creep along at elephantine pace to serve the needs of others only; cargo boats make no progress at all—that is the owners' concern.

On the third day of Nagendra's journey clouds arose and gradually covered the sky. The river became black, the tree-tops drooped, the paddy birds flew aloft, the water became motionless. Nagendra ordered the *manji* (boatman) to run the boat in shore and make it fast. At that moment the steersman, Rahamat Mullah, was saying his prayers, so he made no answer. Rahamat knew nothing of his business. His mother's father's sister was the daughter of a boatman; on that plea he had become a hanger-on of boatmen, and accident favoured his wishes; but he learned nothing, his work was done as fate willed. Rahamat was not backward in speech, and when his prayers were ended he turned to the Babu and said, " Do not be alarmed, sir, there is no cause for fear." Rahamat was thus brave because the shore was close at hand, and could be reached without delay, and in a few minutes the boat was secured.

Surely the gods must have had a quarrel with

Rahamat Mullah, for a great storm came up quickly. First came the wind; then the wind, having wrestled for some moments with the boughs of the trees, called to its brother the rain, and the two began a fine game. Brother Rain, mounting on brother Wind's shoulders, flew along. The two together, seizing the tree-tops, bent them down, broke the boughs, tore off the creepers, washed away the flowers, cast up the river in great waves, and made a general tumult. One brother flew off with Rahamat Mullah's head-gear; the other made a fountain of his beard. The boatmen lowered the sail, the Babu closed the windows, and the servants put the furniture under shelter.

Nagendra was in a great strait. If, in fear of the storm, he should leave the boat, the men would think him a coward; if he remained he would break his word to Surja Mukhi. Some may ask, What harm if he did ? We know not, but Nagendra thought it harm. At this moment Rahamat Mullah said, " Sir, the rope is old ; I do not know what may happen. The storm has much increased;

it will be well to leave the boat." Accordingly Nagendra got out.

No one can stand on the river bank without shelter in a heavy storm of rain. There was no sign of abatement; therefore Nagendra, thinking it necessary to seek for shelter, set out to walk to the village, which was at some distance from the river, through miry paths. Presently the rain ceased, the wind abated slightly, but the sky was still thickly covered with clouds; therefore both wind and rain might be expected at night. Nagendra went on, not turning back.

Though it was early in the evening, there was thick darkness, because of the clouds. There was no sign of village, house, plain, road, or river; but the trees, being surrounded by myriads of fire-flies, looked like artificial trees studded with diamonds. The lightning goddess also still sent quick flashes through the now silent black and white clouds. A woman's anger does not die away suddenly. The assembled frogs, rejoicing in the newly fallen rain, held high festival; and if you listened attentively the voice of the cricket might be heard, like

the undying crackle of Ravana's[1] funeral pyre.
Amid the sounds might be distinguished the fall
of the rain-drops on the leaves of the trees, and
that of the leaves into the pools beneath; the
noise of jackals' feet on the wet paths, occasionally
that of the birds on the trees shaking the water
from their drenched feathers, and now and then
the moaning of the almost subdued wind. Presently Nagendra saw a light in the distance.
Traversing the flooded earth, drenched by the
drippings from the trees, and frightening away the
jackals, he approached the light; and on nearing
it with much difficulty, saw that it proceeded from
an old brick-built house, the door of which was
open. Leaving his servant outside, Nagendra
entered the house, which he found in a frightful
condition.

It was not quite an ordinary house, but it had
no sign of prosperity. The door-frames were
broken and dirty; there was no trace of human
occupation—only owls, mice, reptiles, and insects

[1] King of Lanka (Ceylon), whose remains were to burn without ceasing.

gathered there. The light came only from one side. Nagendra saw some articles of furniture for human use; but everything indicated poverty. One or two cooking vessels, a broken oven, three or four brass dishes—these were the sole ornaments of the place. The walls were black; spiders' webs hung in the corners; cockroaches, spiders, lizards, and mice, scampered about everywhere. On a dilapidated bedstead lay an old man who seemed to be at death's door; his eyes were sunk, his breath hurried, his lips trembling. By the side of his bed stood an earthen lamp upon a fragment of brick taken from the ruins of the house. In it the oil was deficient; so also was it in the body of the man. Another lamp shone by the bedside—a girl of faultlessly fair face, of soft, starry beauty.

Whether because the light from the oil-less lamp was dim, or because the two occupants of the house were absorbed in thinking of their approaching separation, Nagendra's entrance was unseen. Standing in the doorway, he heard the last sorrowful words that issued from the mouth of the old man. These two, the old man and the young girl, were friendless in this densely-peopled world. Once they had had wealth, relatives, men and maid servants—abundance of all kinds; but by the fickleness of fortune, one after another, all had gone. The mother of the family, seeing the faces of her son and daughter daily fading like the dew-drenched lotus from the pinch of poverty, had early sunk upon the bed of death. All the other stars had been extinguished with that moon. The support of the race, the jewel of his mother's eye, the hope of his father's age, even he had been laid on the pyre before his father's eyes. No one remained save the old man and this enchanting girl. They dwelt in this ruined, deserted house in the midst of the forest. Each was to the other the only helper.

Kunda Nandini was of marriageable age; but she was the staff of her father's blindness, his only bond to this world. While he lived he could give her up to no one. "There are but a few more days; if I give away Kunda where can I abide?" were the old man's thoughts when the question of giving her in marriage arose in his mind. Had it never occurred to him to ask himself what would become of Kunda when his summons came? Now the messenger of death stood at his bedside; he was about to leave the world; where would Kunda be on the morrow?

The deep, indescribable suffering of this thought expressed itself in every failing breath. Tears streamed from his eyes, ever restlessly closing and opening, while at his head sat the thirteen-year-old girl, like a stone figure, firmly looking into her father's face, covered with the shadows of death. Forgetting herself, forgetting to think where she would go on the morrow, she gazed only on the face of her departing parent. Gradually the old man's utterance became obscure, the breath left the throat, the eyes lost their light, the suffering soul obtained release from pain. In that dark place, by that glimmering lamp, the solitary Kunda Nandini, drawing her father's dead body on to her lap, remained sitting. The night was extremely dark; even now rain-drops fell, the leaves of the trees rustled, the wind moaned, the windows of the ruined house flapped noisily. In the house, the fitful light of the lamp flickered momentarily on the face of the dead, and again left it in darkness. The lamp had long been exhausted of oil; now, after two or three flashes, it went out. Then Nagendra, with noiseless steps, went forth from the doorway.

CHAPTER II.

"COMING EVENTS CAST THEIR SHADOWS BEFORE."

T was night. In the ruined house Kunda Nandini sat by her father's corpse. She called "Father!" No one made reply. At one moment Kunda thought her father slept, again that he was dead, but she could not bring that thought clearly into her mind. At length she could no longer call, no longer think. The fan still moved in her hand in the direction where her father's once living body now lay dead. At length she resolved that he slept, for if he were dead what would become of her?

After days and nights of watching amid such sorrow, sleep fell upon her. In that exposed, bitterly cold house, the palm-leaf fan in her hand, Kunda Nandini rested her head upon her arm, more beauteous than the lotus-stalk, and slept; and in her sleep she saw a vision. It seemed as if the night were bright and clear, the sky of a pure blue—that glorious blue when the moon is encircled by a halo. Kunda had never seen the halo so large as it seemed in her vision. The light was splendid, and refreshing to the eyes. But in the midst of that magnificent halo there was no moon; in its place Kunda saw the figure of a goddess of unparalleled brilliance. It seemed as if this brilliant goddess-ruled halo left the upper sky and descended gradually lower, throwing out a thousand rays of light, until it stood over Kunda's head. Then she saw that the central beauty, crowned with golden hair, and decked with jewels, had the form of a woman. The beautiful, compassionate face had a loving smile upon its lips. Kunda recognized, with mingled joy and fear, in this compassionate being the features of her long-dead mother. The shining, loving being, raising Kunda from the earth, took her into her bosom, and the orphan girl could for a long period do nought but utter the sweet word " Mother! "

Then the shining figure, kissing Kunda's face, said to her: "Child, thou hast suffered much, and I know thou hast yet more to suffer; thou so young, thy tender frame cannot endure such sorrow. Therefore abide not here; leave the earth and come with me."

Kunda seemed to reply: " Whither shall I go ? "

Then the mother, with uplifted finger indicating the shining constellations, answered, " There ! "

Kunda seemed, in her dream, to gaze into the timeless, shoreless ocean of stars, and to say, " I have no strength; I cannot go so far."

Hearing this, the mother's kind and cheerful but somewhat grave face saddened, her brows knitted a little, as she said in grave, sweet tones:

" Child, follow thy own will, but it would be

well for thee to go with me. The day will come when thou wilt gaze upon the stars, and long bitterly to go thither. I will once more appear to thee; when, bowed to the dust with affliction, thou rememberest me, and weepest to come to me, I will return. Then do thou come. But now do thou, looking on the horizon, follow the design of my finger. I will show thee two human figures. These two beings are in this world the arbiters of thy destiny. If possible, when thou meetest them turn away as from venomous snakes. In their paths walk thou not."

Then the shining figure pointed to the opposite sky. Kunda, following the indication, saw traced on the blue vault the figure of a man more beautiful than a god. Beholding his high, capacious forehead, his sincere kindly glance, his swan-like neck a little bent, and other traits of a fine man, no one would have believed that from him there was anything to be feared.

Then the figure dissolving as a cloud in the sky, the mother said—

"Forget not this god-like form. Though benevolent, he will be the cause of thy misery; therefore avoid him as a snake."

Again pointing to the heavens she continued—"Look hither."

Kunda, looking, saw a second figure sketched before her, not this time that of a man, but a young woman of bright complexion and lotus-shaped eyes. At this sight she felt no fear; but the mother said—

"This dark figure in a woman's dress is a *Rakshasi*.[1] When thou seest her, flee from her."

As she thus spoke the heavens suddenly became dark, the halo disappeared from the sky, and with it the bright figure in its midst.

Then Kunda awoke from her sleep.

Nagendra went to the village, the name of which he heard was Jhunjhunpur. At his recommendation and expense, some of the villagers performed the necessary rites for the dead, one of the female neighbours remaining with the bereaved girl. When Kunda saw that they had taken her father

[1] A female demon.

away, she became convinced of his death, and gave way to ceaseless weeping.

In the morning the neighbour returned to her own house, but sent her daughter Champa to comfort Kunda Nandini.

Champa was of the same age as Kunda, and her friend. She strove to divert her mind by talking of various matters, but she saw that Kunda did not attend. She wept constantly, looking up every now and then into the sky as though in expectation.

Champa jestingly asked, "What do you see that you look into the sky a hundred times?"

Kunda replied, "My mother appeared to me yesterday, and bade me go with her, but I feared to do so; now I mourn that I did not. If she came again I would go: therefore I look constantly into the sky."

Champa said, "How can the dead return?"

To which Kunda replied by relating her vision.

Greatly astonished, Champa asked, "Are you acquainted with the man and woman whose forms you saw in the sky?"

"No, I had never seen them. There cannot be anywhere a man so handsome; I never saw such beauty."

On rising in the morning, Nagendra inquired of the people in the village what would become of the dead man's daughter, where she would live, and whether she had any relatives. He was told that there was no dwelling-place for her, and that she had no relatives.

Then Nagendra said, "Will not some of you receive her and give her in marriage? I will pay the expense, and so long as she remains amongst you I will pay so much a month for her board and lodging."

If he had offered ready money many would have consented to his proposal; but after he had gone away Kunda would have been reduced to servitude, or turned out of the house. Nagendra did not act in so foolish a manner; therefore, money not being forthcoming, no one consented to his suggestion.

At length one, seeing him at the end of his

resources, observed: "A sister of her mother's lives at Sham Bazar; Binod Ghosh is the husband's name. You are on you way to Calcutta; if you take her with you and place her with her aunt, then this *Kaystha* girl will be cared for, and you will have done your duty to your caste."

Seeing no other plan, Nagendra adopted this suggestion, and sent for Kunda to acquaint her with the arrangement.

Champa accompanied Kunda. As they were coming, Kunda, seeing Nagendra from afar, suddenly stood still like one stunned. Her feet refused to move; she stood looking at him with eyes full of astonishment.

Champa asked, "Why do you stand thus?"

Kunda, pointing with her finger, said, "It is he!"

"He! Who?" said Champa.

"He whom last night my mother pictured in the heavens."

Then Champa also stood frightened and astonished. Seeing that the girls shrank from approaching, Nagendra came near and explained everything. Kunda was unable to reply; she could only gaze with eyes full of surprise.

CHAPTER III.

OF MANY SUBJECTS.

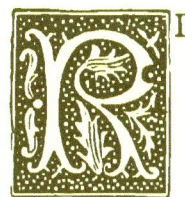ELUCTANTLY did Nagendra Natha take Kunda with him to Calcutta. On arriving there he made much search for her aunt's husband, but he found no one in Sham Bazar named Binod Ghosh. He found a Binod Das, who admitted no relationship. Thus Kunda remained as a burthen upon Nagendra.

Nagendra had one sister, younger than himself, named Kamal Mani, whose father-in-law's house was in Calcutta. Her husband's name was Srish Chandra Mittra. Srish Babu was accountant in the house of Plunder, Fairly, and Co. It was a great house, and Srish Chandra was wealthy. He was much attached to his brother-in-law. Nagendra took Kunda Nandini thither, and imparted her story to Kamal Mani.

Kamal was about eighteen years of age. In features she resembled Nagendra; both brother and sister were very handsome. But, in addition to her beauty, Kamal was famed for her learning. Nagendra's father, engaging an English teacher, had had Kamal Mani and Surja Mukhi well instructed. Kamal's mother-in-law was living, but she dwelt in Srish Chandra's ancestral home. In Calcutta Kamal Mani was house-mistress.

When he had finished the story of Kunda Nandini, Nagendra said, "Unless you will keep her here, there is no place for her. Later, when I return home, I will take her to Govindpur with me."

Kamal was very mischievous. When Nagendra had turned away, she snatched up Kunda in her arms and ran off with her. A tub of not very hot water stood in an adjoining room, and suddenly

Kamal threw Kunda into it. Kunda was quite frightened. Then Kamal, laughing, took some scented soap and proceeded to wash Kunda. An attendant, seeing Kamal thus employed, bustled up, saying, "I will do it! I will do it!" but Kamal, sprinkling some of the hot water over the woman, sent her running away. Kamal having bathed and rubbed Kunda, she appeared like a dew-washed lotus. Then Kamal, having robed her in a beautiful white garment, dressed her hair with scented oil, and decorated her with ornaments, said to her: "Now go and salute the *Dada Babu* (elder brother), and return, but mind you do not thus to the master of the house; if he should see you he will want to marry you."

Nagendra Natha wrote Kunda's history to Surja Mukhi. Also when writing to an intimate friend of his living at a distance, named Hara Deb Ghosal, he spoke of Kunda in the following terms:

"Tell me what you consider to be the age of beauty in woman. You will say after forty, because your Brahmini is a year or two more than that. The girl Kunda, whose history I have given you, is thirteen. On looking at her, it seems as if that were the age of beauty. The sweetness and simplicity that precede the budding-time of youth are never seen afterwards. This Kunda's simplicity is astonishing; she understands nothing. To-day she even wished to run into the streets to play with the boys. On being forbidden, she was much frightened, and desisted. Kamal is teaching her, and says she shows much aptitude in learning, but she does not understand other things. For instance, her large blue eyes—eyes swimming ever like the autumn lotus in clear water—these two eyes may be fixed upon my face, but they say nothing. I lose my senses gazing on them; I cannot explain better. You will laugh at this history of my mental stability; but if I could place you in front of those eyes, I should see what your firmness is worth. Up to this time I have been unable to determine what those eyes are like. I have not seen them look twice the same; I think there are no other such eyes in the world, they seem as if they scarcely saw the things of earth, but were ever seeking something in space. It is not that Kunda is faultlessly beautiful. Her features, if compared with those of many others, would not be highly praised; yet I think I never saw such rare beauty. It is as if there were in Kunda Nandini something not of this world, as though she were not made of flesh and blood, but of moonbeams and the scent of flowers. Nothing presents itself to my mind at this moment to which to liken her. Incomparable being! her whole person seems to breathe peace. If in some clear pool you have observed the sheen produced by the rays of the autumn moon, you have seen something resembling her. I can think of no other simile."

Surja Mukhi's reply to Nagendra's letter came in a few days. It was after this manner:

"I know not what fault your servant has committed. If it is necessary you should stay so long in Calcutta, why am I not with you to attend upon you? This is my earnest wish; the moment I receive your consent, I will set out.

"In picking up a little girl, have you forgotten me? Many unripe things are esteemed. People like green guavas, and green cucumbers; green cocoa-nuts are cooling. This low-born female is also, I think, very young, else in meeting with her why should you forget me? Joking apart, have you given up all right over this girl? if not, I beg her from you. It is my business to arrange for her. In whatever becomes yours I have the right to share, but in this case I see your sister has entire possession. Still, I shall not vex myself much if Kamal usurps my rights.

"Do you ask what do I want with the girl? I wish to give her in marriage with Tara Charan. You know how much I have sought for a suitable wife for him. If Providence has sent us a good girl, do not disappoint me. If Kamal will give her up, bring Kunda Nandini with you when you come. I have written to Kamal also recommending this. I am having ornaments fashioned, and am making other preparations for the marriage. Do not linger in Calcutta. Is it not true that if a man stays six months in that city he becomes quite stupid? If you design to marry Kunda, bring her with you, and I will give her to you.

Only say that you propose to marry her, and I will arrange the marriage-basket."

Who Tara Charan was will be explained later. Whoever he was, both Nagendra and Kamal Mani consented to Surja Mukhi's proposal. Therefore it was resolved that when Nagendra went home Kunda Nandini should accompany him. Every one consented with delight, and Kamal also prepared some ornaments. How blind is man to the future! Some years later there came a day when Nagendra and Kamal Mani bowed to the dust, and, striking their foreheads in grief, murmured: "In how evil a moment did we find Kunda Nandini! in how evil an hour did we agree to Surja Mukhi's letter!" Now Kamal Mani, Surja Mukhi, and Nagendra, together have sowed the poison seed; later they will all repent it with wailing.

Causing his boat to be got ready, Nagendra returned to Govindpur with Kunda Nandini. Kunda had almost forgotten her dream; while journeying with Nagendra it recurred to her memory, but thinking of his benevolent face and kindly character, Kunda could not believe that any harm would come to her from him. In like manner there are many insects who, seeing a destructive flame, enter therein.

CHAPTER IV.

TARA CHARAN.

HE Poet Kalidas was supplied with flowers by a *Malini* (flower-girl). He, being a poor Brahmin, could not pay for the flowers, but in place of that he used to read some of his own verses to the *Malini*. One day there bloomed in the *Malini's* tank a lily of unparalleled beauty. Plucking it, the *Malini* offered it to Kalidas. As a reward the poet read to her some verses from the *Megha Duta* (Cloud Messenger). That poem is an ocean of wit, but every one knows that its opening lines are tasteless. The *Malini* did not relish them, and being annoyed she rose to go.

The poet asked: "Oh! friend *Malini*, are you going?"

"Your verses have no flavour," replied the *Malini*.

"*Malini!* you will never reach heaven."

"Why so?"

"There is a staircase to heaven. By ascending millions of steps heaven is reached. My poem has also a staircase; these tasteless verses are the steps. If you can't climb these few steps, how will you ascend the heavenly ladder?"

The *Malini* then, in fear of losing heaven through the Brahmin's curse, listened to the *Megha Duta* from beginning to end. She admired the poem; and next day, binding a wreath of flowers in the name of Cupid, she crowned the poet's temples therewith.

This ordinary poem of mine is not heaven; neither has it a staircase of a million steps. Its flavour is faint and the steps are few. These few tasteless chapters are the staircase. If among my readers there is one of the *Malini's* disposition, I warn him that without climbing these steps he will not arrive at the pith of the story.

Surja Mukhi's father's house was in Konnagar. Her father was a *Kaystha* of good position. He was cashier in some house at Calcutta. Surja Mukhi was his only child. In her infancy a *Kaystha* widow named Srimati lived in her father's house as a servant, and looked after Surja Mukhi. Srimati had one child named Tara Charan, of the same age as Surja Mukhi. With him Surja Mukhi had played, and on account of this childish association she felt towards him the affection of a sister.

Srimati was a beautiful woman, and therefore soon fell into trouble. A wealthy man of the village, of evil character, having cast his eyes upon her, she forsook the house of Surja Mukhi's father. Whither she went no one exactly knew, but she did not return. Tara Charan, forsaken by his mother, remained in the house of Surja Mukhi's father, who was a very kind-hearted man, and brought up this deserted boy as his own child; not keeping him in slavery as an unpaid servant, but having him taught to read and write. Tara Charan learned English at a free mission-school.

Afterwards Surja Mukhi was married, and some years later her father died. By this time Tara Charan had learned English after a clumsy fashion, but he was not qualified for any business. Rendered homeless by the death of Surja Mukhi's father, he went to her house. At her instigation Nagendra opened a school in the village, and Tara Charan was appointed master. Nowadays, by means of the grant-in-aid system in many villages, sleek-haired, song-singing, harmless Master Babus appear; but at that time such a being as a Master Babu was scarcely to be seen. Consequently, Tara Charan appeared as one of the village gods; especially as it was known in the bazaar that he had read the *Citizen of the World*, the *Spectator*, and three books of *Euclid*. On account of these gifts he was received into the *Brahmo Samaj* of Debendra Babu, the zemindar of Debipur, and reckoned as one of that Babu's retinue.

Tara Charan wrote many essays on widow-marriage, on the education of women, and against idol-worship; read them weekly in the *Samaj*, and delivered many discourses beginning with "Oh, most merciful God!" Some of these he took from the *Tattwa Bodhini*,[1] and some he caused to be written for him by the school *pandit*. He was for ever preaching: "Abandon idol-worship, give choice in marriage, give women education; why do you keep them shut up in a cage? let women come out." There was a special cause for this liberality on the subject of women, inasmuch as in his own house there was no woman. Up to this time he had not married. Surja Mukhi had made great efforts to get him married, but as his mother's story was known in Govindpur, no respectable *Kaystha* consented to give him his daughter. Many a common, disreputable *Kaystha* girl he might have had; but Surja Mukhi, regarding Tara Charan as a brother, would not give her consent, since she did not choose to call such a girl sister-in-law. While she was seeking for a respectable *Kaystha* girl, Nagendra's letter came, describing Kunda Nandini's gifts and beauty. She resolved to give her to Tara Charan in marriage.

[1] A religious periodical published in Calcutta.

CHAPTER V.

OH! LOTUS-EYED, WHO ART THOU?

UNDA arrived safely with Nagendra at Govindpur. At the sight of Nagendra's dwelling she became speechless with wonder, for she had never seen one so grand. There were three divisions without and three within. Each division was a large city. The outer *mahal* (division) was entered by an iron gate, and was surrounded on all sides by a handsome lofty iron railing. From the gate a broad, red, well-metalled path extended, on each side of which were beds of fresh grass that would have formed a paradise for cows. In the midst of

each plat was a circle of shrubs, all blooming with variously coloured flowers. In front rose the lofty demi-upper-roomed *boita khana* (reception-hall), approached by a broad flight of steps, the verandah of which was supported by massive fluted pillars. The floor of the lower part of this house was of marble. Above the parapet, in its centre, an enormous clay lion, with dependent mane, hung out its red tongue. This was Nagendra's *boita khana*. To left and right of the grass plats stood a row of one-storied buildings, containing on one side the *daftar khana* (accountant's office) and *kacheri* (court-house); on the other the storehouse, treasury, and servants' dwellings. On both sides of the gate were the doorkeepers' lodges. This first *mahal* was named the *kacheri bari* (house of business); the next to it was the *puja mahal* (division for worship). The large hall of worship formed one side of the *puja mahal*; on the other three sides were two-storied houses. No one lived in this *mahal*. At the festival of Durga it was thronged; but now grass sprouted between the tiles of the court, pigeons frequented the halls, the houses were full of furniture, and the doors were kept locked. Beside this was the *thakur bari* (room assigned to the family deity): in it on one side was the temple of the gods, the handsome stone-built dancing-hall; on the remaining sides, the kitchen for the gods, the dwelling-rooms of the priests, and a guest-house. In this *mahal* there was no lack of people. The tribe of priests, with garlands on their necks and sandal-wood marks on their foreheads; a troop of cooks; people bearing baskets of flowers for the altars; some bathing the gods, some ringing bells, chattering, pounding sandal-wood, cooking; men and women servants bearing water, cleaning floors, washing rice, quarrelling with the cooks. In the guest-house an ascetic, with ash-smeared, loose hair, is lying sleeping; one with upraised arm (stiffened thus through years) is distributing drugs and charms to the servants of the house; a white-bearded, red-robed *Brahmachari*, swinging his chaplet of beads, is reading from a manuscript copy of the *Bhagavat-gita* in the *Nagari* character; holy mendicants are quarrelling for their share of *ghi* and flour. Here a company of emaciated *Boiragis*, with wreaths of *tulsi* (a sacred plant) round their necks and the marks of their religion painted on their foreheads, the bead fastened into the knot of hair on their heads shaking with each movement, are beating the drums as they sing:

> "I could not get the opportunity to speak,
> The elder brother Dolai was with me."

The wives of the *Boiragis*, their hair braided in a manner pleasing to their husbands, are singing the tune of *Govinda Adhi Kari* to the accompaniment of the tambourine. Young *Boisnavis* singing with elder women of the same class, the middle-aged trying to bring their voices into unison with those of the old. In the midst of the courtyard idle boys fighting, and abusing each other's parents.

These three were the outer *mahals*. Behind these came the three inner ones. The inner *mahal* behind the *kacheri bari* was for Nagendra's private use. In that only himself, his wife, and their personal attendants were allowed; also the furniture for their use. This place was new, built by Nagendra himself, and very well arranged. Next to it, and behind the *puja bari*, came another *mahal;* this was old, ill-built, the rooms low, small, and dirty. Here was a whole city-full of female relations, mother's sister and mother's cousin, father's sister and cousin; mother's widowed sister, mother's married sister; father's sister's son's wife, mother's sister's son's daughter. All these female relatives cawing day and night like a set of crows in a banian tree; at every moment screams, laughter, quarrelling, bad reasoning, gossip, reproach, the scuffling of boys, the crying of girls. "Bring water!" "Give the clothes!" "Cook the rice!" "The child does not eat!" "Where is the milk?" etc., is heard as an ocean of confused sounds. Next to it, behind the *Thakur bari*, was the cook-house. Here a woman, having placed the rice-pot on the fire, gathering up her feet, sits gossiping with her neighbour on the details of her son's marriage. Another, endeavouring to light a fire with green wood, her eyes smarting with the smoke, is abusing the *gomashta* (factor), and producing abundant proof that he has supplied this wet wood to pocket part of the price. Another beauty, throwing fish into the hot oil, closes her eyes and twists her ten fingers, making a grimace, for oil leaping forth has burnt her skin. One having bathed her long hair, plentifully besmeared with oil, braiding it in a curve on the temples and fastening it in a knot on the top of her head, stirs the pulse cooking in an earthen pot, like Krishna prodding the cows with a stick. Here Bami, Kaymi, Gopal's mother, Nipal's mother, are shredding with a big knife vegetable pumpkins, brinjals, the sound of the cutting steel mingling with abuse of the neighbours, of the masters, of everybody: that Golapi has become a widow very young; that Chandi's husband is a great drunkard; that Koylash's husband has secured a fine appointment as writer to the *Darogah*; that there could not be in the world such a flying journey as that of Gopal, nor such a wicked child as Parvati's; how the English must be of the race of *Ravan* (the ten-headed king of Ceylon); how *Bhagirati* had brought *Ganga*; how Sham Biswas was the lover of the daughter of the

Bhattacharjyas; with many other subjects. A dark, stout-bodied woman, placing a large *bonti* (a fish-cutter) on a heap of ashes in the court, is cutting fish; the kites, frightened at her gigantic size and her quick-handedness, keeping away, yet now and again darting forward to peck at the fish. Here a white-haired woman is bringing water; there one with powerful hand is grinding spices. Here, in the storehouse, a servant, a cook, and the storekeeper are quarrelling together; the storekeeper maintaining, "The *ghi* (clarified butter) I have given is the right quantity;" the cook disputing it; the servant saying, "We could manage with the quantity you give if you left the storehouse unlocked." In the hope of receiving doles of rice, many children and beggars with their dogs are sitting waiting. The cats do not flatter any one; they watch their opportunity, steal in, and help themselves. Here a cow without an owner is feasting with closed eyes upon the husks of pumpkins, other vegetables, and fruit.

Behind these three inner *mahals* is the flower-garden; and further yet a broad tank, blue as the sky. This tank is walled in. The inner house (the women's) has three divisions, and in the flower-garden is a private path, and at each end of the path two doors; these doors are private, they give entrance to the three *mahals* of the inner house. Outside the house are the stables, the elephant-house, the kennels, the cow-house, the aviaries, etc.

Kunda Nandini, full of astonishment at Nagendra's unbounded wealth, was borne in a palanquin to the inner apartments, where she saluted Surja Mukhi, who received her with a blessing.

Having recognized in Nagendra the likeness of the man she had seen in her dream, Kunda Nandini doubted whether his wife would not resemble the female figure she had seen later; but the sight of Surja Mukhi removed this doubt. Surja Mukhi was of a warm, golden colour, like the full moon; the figure in the dream was dark. Surja Mukhi's eyes were beautiful, but not like those in the dream. They were long deer-eyes, extending to the side hair; the eye-brows joined in a beautiful curve over the dilated, densely black pupils, full but steady. The eyes of the dark woman in the dream were not so enchanting. Then Surja Mukhi's features were not similar. The dream figure was dwarfish; Surja Mukhi rather tall, her figure swaying with the beauty of the honeysuckle creeper. The dream figure was beautiful, but Surja Mukhi was a hundredfold more so. The dream figure was not more than twenty years of age; Surja Mukhi was nearly twenty-six. Kunda saw clearly that there was no resemblance between the two. Surja Mukhi conversed pleasantly with Kunda, and summoned the attendants, to the chief among whom she said, " This is Kunda with whom I shall give Tara Charan in marriage ; therefore see that you treat her as my brother's wife."

The servant expressed her assent, and took Kunda aside with her to another place. At sight of her Kunda's flesh crept; a cold moisture came over her from head to foot. The female figure which Kunda in her dream had seen her mother's fingers trace upon the heavens, this servant was that lotus-eyed, dark-complexioned woman.

Kunda, agitated with fear, breathing with difficulty, asked, " Who are you ? "

The servant answered, " My name is Hira."

CHAPTER VI.

THE READER HAS CAUSE FOR GREAT DISPLEASURE.

T this point the reader will be much annoyed. It is a custom with novelists to conclude with a wedding, but we are about to begin with the marriage of Kunda Nandini. By another custom that has existed from ancient times, whoever shall marry the heroine must be extremely handsome, adorned with all virtues, himself a hero, and devoted to his mistress. Poor Tara Charan possessed no such advantages; his beauty consisted in a copper-tinted complexion and a snub nose; his heroism found exercise only in the

schoolroom; and as for his love, I cannot say how much he had for Kunda Nandini, but he had some for a pet monkey.

However that may be, soon after Kunda Nandini's arrival at the house of Nagendra she was married to Tara Charan. Tara Charan took home his beautiful wife; but in marrying a beautiful wife he brought himself into a difficulty.

The reader will remember that Tara Charan had delivered some essays in the house of Debendra Babu on the subjects of women's education and the opening of the zenana. In the discussions that ensued, the Master Babu had said vauntingly: "Should the opportunity ever be given me, I will be the first to set an example of reform in these matters. Should I marry, I will bring my wife out into society."

Now he was married, and the fame of Kunda's beauty had spread through the district. All the neighbours now, quoting an old song, said, "Where now is his pledge?" Debendra said, "What, are you now also in the troop of old fools? Why do you not introduce us to your wife?"

Tara Charan was covered with shame; he could not escape from Debendra's banter and taunts. He consented to allow Debendra to make the acquaintance of his wife. Then fear arose lest Surja Mukhi should be displeased. A year passed in evasion and procrastination; when, seeing that this could be carried on no longer, he made an excuse that his house was in need of repair, and sent Kunda Nandini to Nagendra's house. When the repairs of the house were completed, Kunda Nandini returned home. A few days after, Debendra, with some of his friends, called upon Tara Charan, and jeered him for his false boasting. Driven thus, as it were, into a corner, Tara Charan persuaded Kunda Nandini to dress in suitable style, and brought her forth to converse with Debendra Babu. How could she do so? She remained standing veiled before him for a few seconds, then fled weeping. But Debendra was enchanted with her youthful grace and beauty. He never forgot it.

Soon after that, some kind of festival was held in Debendra's house, and a little girl was sent thence to Kunda to invite her attendance. But Surja Mukhi hearing of this, forbade her to accept the invitation, and she did not go. Later, Debendra again going to Tara Charan's house, had an interview with Kunda. Surja Mukhi hearing of this through others, gave to Tara Charan such a scolding, that from that time Debendra's visits were stopped.

In this manner three years passed after the marriage; then Kunda Nandini became a widow. Tara Charan died of fever. Surja Mukhi took Kunda to live with her, and selling the house she had given to Tara Charan, gave the proceeds in Government paper to Kunda.

The reader is no doubt much displeased, but in fact the tale is only begun. Of the poison tree the seed only has thus far been sown.

CHAPTER VII.

HARIDASI BOISNAVI.

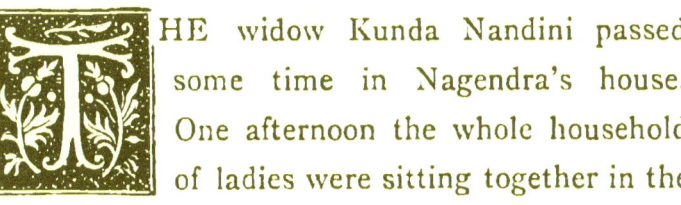HE widow Kunda Nandini passed some time in Nagendra's house. One afternoon the whole household of ladies were sitting together in the older division of the house, all occupied according to their tastes in the simple employment of village women. All ages were there, from the youngest girl to the grey-haired woman. One was binding another's hair, the other suffering it to be bound; one submitting to have her white hairs extracted, another extracting them by the aid of a grain of rice; one beauty sewing together shreds of cloth into a quilt for her boy, another suckling her

child; one lovely being dressing the plaits of her hair; another beating her child, who now cried aloud, now quietly sobbed, by turns. Here one is sewing carpet-work, another leaning over it in admiring examination. There one of artistic taste, thinking of some one's marriage, is drawing a design on the wooden seats to be used by the bridal pair. One learned lady is reading Dasu Rai's poetry. An old woman is delighting the ears of her neighbours with complaints of her son; a humorous young one, in a voice half bursting with laughter, relates in the ears of her companions whose husbands are absent some jocose story of her husband's, to beguile the pain of separation. Some are reproaching the *Grihini* (house-mistress), some the *Korta* (master), some the neighbours; some reciting their own praises. She who may have received a gentle scolding in the morning from Surja Mukhi on account of her stupidity, is bringing forward many examples of her remarkable acuteness of understanding. She in whose cooking the flavours can never be depended upon, is dilating at great length upon her proficiency in the art. She whose husband is proverbial in the village for his ignorance, is astounding her companions by her praises of his superhuman learning. She whose children are dark and repulsive-looking, is pluming herself on having given birth to jewels of beauty. Surja Mukhi was not of the company. She was a little proud, and did not sit much with these people; if she came amongst them her presence was a restraint upon the enjoyment of the rest. All feared her somewhat, and were reserved towards her. Kunda Nandini associated with them; she was amongst them now, teaching a little boy his letters at his mother's request. During the lesson the pupil's eyes were fixed upon the sweetmeat in another child's hand, consequently his progress was not great. At this moment there appeared amongst them a *Boisnavi* (female mendicant), exclaiming, "*Jai Radhika!*"[1] (Victory to Radhika).

A constant stream of guests was served in Nagendra's *Thakur bari*, and every Sunday quantities of rice were distributed in the same

[1] Wife of Krishna.

place, but neither *Boisnavis* nor others were allowed to come to the women's apartments to beg; accordingly, on hearing the cry "*Jai Radha!*" in these forbidden precincts, one of the inmates exclaimed: "What, woman! do you venture to intrude here? go to the *Thakur bari*." But even as she spoke, turning to look at the *Boisnavi*, she could not finish her speech, but said instead: "Oh, ma, what *Boisnavi* are you?"

Looking up, all saw with astonishment that the *Boisnavi* was young and of exceeding beauty; in that group of beautiful women there was none, excepting Kunda Nandini, so beautiful as she. Her trembling lips, well-formed nose, large lotus-eyes, pencilled brows, smooth, well-shaped forehead, arms like the lotus-stalk, and complexion like the *champak* flower, were rare among women. But had there been present any critic of loveliness, he would have said there was a want of sweetness in her beauty, while in her walk and in her movements there was a masculine character.

The *sandal* mark[1] on the *Boisnavi*'s nose was

[1] The caste mark, made with sandal-wood powder.

long and fine, her hair was braided, she wore a *sari* with a coloured border, and carried a small tambourine in her hand. She wore brass bracelets, and over them others made of black glass.

One of the elder women addressed her saying, "Who are you?"

The *Boisnavi* replied, "My name is Haridasi. Will the ladies like a song?"

The cry, "Yes, yes! sing!" sounded on all sides from old and young. Raising her tambourine, the *Boisnavi* seated herself near the ladies, where Kunda was teaching the little boy. Kunda was very fond of music; on hearing that the *Boisnavi* would sing she came nearer. Her pupil seized the opportunity to snatch the sweetmeat from the other child's hand, and eat it himself.

The *Boisnavi* asking what she should sing, the listeners gave a number of different orders. One called for the strains of *Govinda Adhikari*, another *Gopale Ure*. She who was reading Dasu Rai's poem desired to have it sung. Two or three asked for the old stories about Krishna; they were divided as to whether they would hear about the companions or about the separation. Some wanted to hear of his herding the cows in his youth. One shameless girl called out, "If you do not sing such and such a passage I will not listen." One mere child, by way of teaching the *Boisnavi*, sang some nonsensical syllables. The *Boisnavi*, listening to the different demands, gave a momentary glance at Kunda, saying: "Have you no commands to give?"

Kunda, ashamed, bent her head smiling, but did not speak aloud; she whispered in the ear of a companion, "Mention some hymn."

The companion said, "Kunda desires that you will sing a hymn." The *Boisnavi* then began a hymn. Kunda, seeing that the *Boisnavi* had neglected all other commands to obey hers, was much abashed. Haridasi, striking gently on her tambourine as if in sport, recited in a gentle voice some few notes like the murmuring of a bee in early spring, or a bashful bride's first loving speech to her husband. Then suddenly she produced from that insignificant tambourine, as though with the fingers of a powerful musician, sounds like the crashing of the clouds in thunder, making the frames of her hearers shrink within them as she sang in tones more melodious than those of the *Apsharas* (celestial singing women).

The ladies, astonished and enchanted, heard the *Boisnavi's* unequalled voice filling the court with sound that ascended to the skies. What could secluded women understand of the method of that singing? An intelligent person would have comprehended that this perfect singing was not due to natural gifts alone. The *Boisnavi*, whoever she might be, had received a thorough scientific training in music, and, though young, she was very proficient.

The *Boisnavi*, having finished her song, was urged by the ladies to sing again. Haridasi, looking with thirsty eyes at Kunda, sang the following song from Krishna's address to Radhika:

THE BOISNAVI'S SONG.

" To see thy beauteous lily face
I come expectant to this place ;
Let me, oh Rai ! thy feet embrace.

> To deprecate thy sullen ire,
> Therefore I come in strange attire;
> Revive me, Radha, kindness speak,
> Clasping thy feet my home I'd seek.
> Of thy fair form to catch a ray
> From door to door with flute I stray;
> When thy soft name it murmurs low
> Mine eyes with sudden tears o'erflow.
> If thou wilt not my pardon speak
> The banks of Jumna's stream I'll seek,
> Will break my flute and yield my life;
> Oh! cease thy wrath, and end the strife.
> The joys of Braj I've cast aside
> A slave before thy feet t' abide;
> Thine anklets round my neck I'll bind,
> In Jumna's stream I'll refuge find."

The song over, the *Boisnavi*, looking at Kunda, said, "Singing has made me thirsty; give me some water."

Kunda brought water in a vessel; but the *Boisnavi* said, "I will not touch your vessel; come near and pour some water into my hands. I was not born a *Boisnavi*." By this she gave it to be understood that she was formerly of some unholy caste, and had since become a *Boisnavi*.

In reply to her words, Kunda went behind her so

as to pour the water into her hands. They were at such a distance from the rest that words spoken gently could not be heard by any of them. Kunda poured the water, and the *Boisnavi* washed her hands and face.

While thus engaged the latter murmured, "Are you not Kunda?"

In astonishment Kunda replied, "Why do you ask?"

"Have you ever seen your mother-in-law?"

"No."

Kunda had heard that her mother-in-law, having lost her good name, had left the place.

Then said the *Boisnavi*: "Your mother-in-law is here now. She is in my house, and is crying bitterly to be allowed to see you for once. She dare not show her face to the mistress of this house. Why should you not go with me to see her? Notwithstanding her fault, she is still your mother-in-law."

Although Kunda was simple, she understood quite well that she should not acknowledge any connection with such a relation. Therefore she merely shook her head at the *Boisnavi's* words and refused her assent. But the *Boisnavi* would not take a refusal; again she urged the matter.

Kunda replied, " I cannot go without the *Grihini's* permission."

This Haridasi forbade. "You must not speak to the house-mistress, she will not let you go; it may be she will send for your *Sasuri* (mother-in-law). In that case your mother-in-law would flee the country."

The more the *Boisnavi* insisted, the more Kunda refused to go without the *Grihini's* permission.

Haridasi having no other resource, said: "Very well, put the thing nicely to the *Grihini;* I will come another day and take you. Mind you put it prudently, and shed some tears also, else she will not consent."

Even to this Kunda did not consent; she would not say either "yes" or "no."

Haridasi, having finished purifying her face and hands, turned to the ladies and asked for contributions. At this moment Surja Mukhi came amongst them, the desultory talk ceased, and the younger women, all pretending some occupation, sat down.

Surja Mukhi, examining the *Boisnavi* from head to foot, inquired, "Who are you?"

An aunt of Nagendra's explained: "She is a *Boisnavi* who came to sing. I never heard such beautiful singing! Will you let her sing for you? Sing something about the goddesses."

Haridasi, having sung a beautiful piece about Sham, Surja Mukhi, enchanted, dismissed her with a handsome present. The *Boisnavi*, making a profound salute, cast one more glance at Kunda and went away. Once out of the range of Surja Mukhi's eyes, she made a few gentle taps on the tambourine, singing softly—

> " Ah, my darling!
> I'll give you honey to eat, golden robes to wear;
> I'll fill your flask with *attar*,
> And your jar with water of rose,
> Your box with spice prepared by my own hand."

The *Boisnavi* being gone, the women could talk of nothing else for some time. First they praised her highly, then began to point out her defects.

Biraj said, "She is beautiful, but her nose is somewhat flat."

Bama remarked, "Her complexion is too pale."

Chandra Mukhi added, "Her hair is like tow."

Kapal said, "Her forehead is too high."

Kamala said, "Her lips are thick."

Harani observed, "Her figure is very wooden."

Pramada added, "The woman's bust is like that of a play actor, it has no grace."

In this manner it soon appeared that the beautiful *Boisnavi* was of unparalleled ugliness.

Then Lalita said, "Whatever her looks may be, she sings beautifully."

But even this was not admitted. Chandra Mukhi said the singing was coarse; Mukta Keshi confirmed this criticism.

Ananga said, "The woman does not know any songs; she could not even give us one of Dasu Rai's songs."

Kanak said, "She does not understand time."

Thus it appeared that Haridasi *Boisnavi* was not only extremely ugly, but that her singing was of the worst description.

CHAPTER VIII.

THE BABU.

ARIDASI *BOISNAVI*, having left the house of the Datta family, went to Debipur. At this place there is a flower-garden surrounded by painted iron railings. It is well stocked with fruit trees and flowering shrubs. In the centre is a tank, upon the edge of which stands a garden-house. Entering a private room in this house, Haridasi threw off her dress. Suddenly that dense mass of hair fell from the head; the locks were borrowed. The bust also fell away; it was made of cloth. After putting on suitable apparel and removing

the *Boisnavi* garments, there stood forth a strikingly handsome young man of about five and twenty years of age. Having no hair on his face he looked quite a youth; in feature he was very handsome. This young man was Debendra Babu, of whom we have before had some slight knowledge.

Debendra and Nagendra were sprung from the same family, but between the two branches there had been feud for successive generations, so that the members of the Debipur family were not on speaking terms with those of Govindpur. From generation to generation there had been lawsuits between the two houses. At length, in an important suit, the grandfather of Nagendra had defeated the grandfather of Debendra, and since that time the Debipur family had been powerless. All their money was swallowed up in law expenses, and the Govindpur house had bought up all their estates. From that time the position of the Debipur family had declined, that of the other increased, the two branches no longer united.

Debendra's father had sought in one way to restore the fallen fortunes of his house. Another zemindar, named Ganesh, dwelt in the Haripur district ; he had one unmarried daughter, Hembati, who was given to Debendra in marriage. Hembati had many virtues; she was ugly, ill-tempered, unamiable, selfish. Up to the time of his marriage with her, Debendra's character had been without stain. He had been very studious, and was by nature steady and truth-loving. But that marriage had been fatal to him. When Debendra came to years of discretion he perceived that on account of his wife's disposition there was no hope of domestic happiness for him. With manhood there arose in him a love for beauty, but in his own house this was denied to him ; with manhood there came a desire for conjugal affection, but the mere sight of the unamiable Hembati quenched the desire. Putting happiness out of the question, Debendra perceived that it would be difficult to stay in the house to endure the venom of Hembati's tongue. One day Hembati poured forth abuse on her husband; he had endured much, he could endure no more, he dragged Hembati by the hair and kicked her. From that day, deserting his home, he went to Calcutta, leaving orders that a small house should be built for him in the garden. Before this occurred the father of Debendra had died, therefore he was independent. In Calcutta he plunged into vicious pursuits to allay his unsatisfied desires, and then strove to wash away his heart's reproaches in wine; after that he ceased to feel any remorse, he took delight in vice.

When he had learned what Calcutta could teach him in regard to luxury, Debendra returned to his native place, and, taking up his abode in the garden-house, gave himself up to the indulgence of his recently acquired tastes. Debendra had learned many peculiar fashions in Calcutta; on returning to Debipur he called himself a Reformer. First he established a *Brahmo Samaj;* many such Brahmos as Tara Charan were attracted to it, and to the speech-making there was no limit. He also thought of opening a female school; but this required too much effort, he could not do it. About widow marriage he was very zealous. One or two such marriages had been arranged, the widows being of low caste; but the credit of these was due, not to him, but to the contracting parties. He had been of one mind with Tara Charan about breaking the chains of the zenana; both had said, "Let women come out." In this matter Debendra was very successful, but then this emancipation had in his mind a special meaning.

When Debendra, on his return from Govindpur, had thrown off his disguise and resumed his natural appearance, he took his seat in the next room. His servant, having prepared the pain-relieving *huka*, placed the snake in front of him. Debendra spent some time in the service of that fatigue-destroying goddess, Tobacco. He is not worthy to be called a man who does not know the luxury of tobacco. Oh, satisfier of the hearts of all! oh, world enchantress! may we ever be devoted to thee! Your vehicles, the *huka*, the pipe, let them ever remain before us. At the mere sight of them we shall obtain heavenly delight. Oh, *huka!* thou that sendest forth volumes of curling smoke, that hast a winding tube shaming the serpent! oh, bowl that beautifies thy top! how graceful are the chains of thy turban;

how great is the beauty of thy curved mouthpiece; how sonorous the murmur of the ice-cool water in thy depths! Oh, world enchantress! oh, soother of the fatigues of man, employer of the idle, comforter of the henpecked husband's heart, encourager of timid dependents, who can know thy glory! Soother of the sorrowing! thou givest courage to the timid, intellect to the stupid, peace to the angry! Oh, bestower of blessings, giver of all happiness, appear in undiminished power in my room! Let your sweet scent increase daily, let your cool waters continue to rumble in your depths, let your mouthpiece ever be glued to my lips!

Pleasure-loving Debendra enjoyed the favour of this great goddess as long as he would, but yet he was not satisfied; he proceeded to worship another great power. In the hand of his servant was displayed a number of straw-covered bottles. Then on that white, soft, spacious bed, a gold-coloured mat being laid, a spirit-stand was placed thereon, and the sunset-coloured liquid goddess poured into the power-giving decanter. A cut-glass tumbler and plated jug served as utensils for worship. From the kitchen a black, ugly priest came, bearing hot dishes of roast mutton and cutlets to take the place of the sacred flowers. Then Debendra, as a devoted worshipper, sat down to perform the rites.

Then came a troop of singers and musicians, and concluded the ceremonies with their music and songs.

At length a young man of about Debendra's age, of a placid countenance, came and sat with him. This was his cousin, Surendra. Surendra was in every respect the opposite of Debendra, yet the latter was much attached to his cousin; he heeded no one in the world but him. Every night Surendra came to see him, but, fearing the wine, he would only sit a few minutes.

When all were gone, Surendra asked Debendra, "How are you to-day?"

"The body," replied Debendra, "is the temple of disease."

"Yours is, especially," said his cousin, "Have you fever to-day?"

"No."

" Is your liver out of order ? "

" It is as before."

" Would it not be better to refrain from these excesses ? "

" What, drinking ? How often will you speak of that ? Wine is my constant companion," said Debendra.

" But why should it be ? " replied Surendra. " Wine was not born with you; you can't take it away with you. Many give it up, why should not you do so ? "

" What have I to gain by giving it up ? Those who do so have some happiness in prospect, and therefore give it up. For me there is no happiness."

" Then to save your life give it up."

" Those to whom life brings happiness may give up wine; but what have I to gain by living ? "

Surendra's eyes filled with tears. Full of love for his friend, he urged :

" Then for my sake give it up."

Tears came into the eyes of Debendra as he

said: "No one but yourself urges me to walk in virtuous paths. If I ever do give it up it will be for your sake, and——"

"And what?"

"If ever I hear that my wife is dead I will give up drink. Otherwise, whether I live or die, I care not."

Surendra, with moist eyes, mentally anathematising Hembati, took his leave.

CHAPTER IX.

SURJA MUKHI'S LETTER.

EAREST Srimati Kamal Mani Dasi, long may you live!

"I am ashamed to address you any longer with a blessing. You have become a woman, and the mistress of a house. Still I cannot think of you otherwise than as my younger sister. I have brought you up to womanhood, I taught you your letters; but now when I see your writing I am ashamed to send this scrawl. But of what use to be ashamed? My day is over; were it not so how should I be in this condition? What condition?—it is a thing I cannot speak of to any one; should I do so there will be sorrow and shame; yet if I do not tell some one of my heart's trouble I cannot endure it. To whom can I speak? You are my beloved sister; except you no one loves me. Also it concerns your brother. I can speak of it to no one but you.

"I have prepared my own funeral pyre. If I had not cared for Kunda Nandini, and she had died, would that have been any loss to me? God cares for so many others—would He not have cared for her? Why did I bring her home to my own destruction! When you saw that unfortunate being she was a child, now she is seventeen or eighteen. I admit she is beautiful; her beauty is fatal to me. If I have any happiness on earth it is in my husband; if I care about anything in this world it is for my husband; if there is any wealth belonging to me it is my husband: this husband Kunda Nandini is snatching from me. If I have a desire on earth it is for my husband's love: of that love Kunda Nandini is cheating me. Do not think evil of your brother; I am not reproaching him. He is virtuous, not even his enemies can find a fault in him. I can see daily that he tries to subdue his heart. Wherever Kunda Nandini may happen to be, from that spot, if possible, he averts his eyes; unless there is absolute necessity he does not speak her name. He is even harsh towards her; I have heard him scold her when she has committed no fault. Then why am I writing all this trash? Should a man ask this question it would be difficult to make him understand, but you being a woman will comprehend. If Kunda Nandini is in his eyes but as other women, why is he so careful not to look towards her? why take such pains to avoid speaking her name? He is conscious of guilt towards Kunda Nandini, therefore he scolds her without cause; that anger is not with her, but with himself; that scolding is not for her, but for himself. This I can understand. I who have been so long devoted to him, who within and without see only him, if I but see his shadow I can tell his thoughts. What can he hide from me? Occasionally when his mind is absent his eyes wander hither and thither; do I not know what they are seeking?

If he meets it, again becoming troubled he withdraws his eyes; can I not understand that? For whose voice is he listening at meal-times when he pauses in the act of carrying food to his mouth? and when Kunda's tones reach his ear, and he hastens to eat his meal, can one not understand that? My beloved always had a gracious countenance; why is he now always so absent-minded? If one speaks to him he does not hear, but gives an absent answer. If, becoming angry, I say, 'May I die?' paying no attention he answers, 'Yes.' If I ask where his thoughts are, he says with his lawsuits; but I know they have no place in his mind; when he speaks of his lawsuits he is always merry. Another point. One day the old women of the neighbourhood were speaking of Kunda Nandini, pitying her young widowhood, her unprotected condition. Your brother came up; from within I saw his eyes fill with tears; he turned away and left them quickly. The other day I engaged a new servant; her name is Kumuda. Sometimes the Babu calls Kumuda; when so doing he often slips out the name Kunda instead of

Kumuda, then how confused he is—why should he be confused? I cannot say he is neglectful of me, or unaffectionate; rather he is more attentive than before, more affectionate. The reason of this I fully understand: he is conscious of fault towards me; but I know that I have no longer a place in his heart. Attention is one thing, love quite another; the difference between these two we women can easily understand.

"There is another amusing matter. A learned *pandit* in Calcutta, named Iswara Chandra Bidya Sagar, has published a book on the marriage of widows. If he who would establish the custom of marrying widows is a *pandit*, then who can be called a dunce? Just now, the Brahman Bhattacharjya bringing the book into the *boita khana*, there was a great discussion.

"After much talk in favour of widow-marriage, the Brahman, taking ten rupees from the Babu for the repairs of the *Tole*,[1] went his way. On the following day Sharbabhoum Thakur replied on the same subject. I had some golden bracelets made

[1] The village school in which Sanscrit is taught.

for his daughter's wedding. No one else was in favour of widow-marriage.

"I have taken up much time in wearying you with my sorrows. Do I not know how vexed you will be? but what can I do, sister? If I do not tell you my sorrows, to whom shall I tell them? I have not said all yet, but hoping for some relief from you has calmed me a little. Say nothing of this to any one; above all, I conjure you, show not this letter to your husband. Will you not come and see me? if you will come now your presence will heal many of my troubles. Send me quickly news of your husband and of your child.

"SURJA MUKHI.

"P.S.—Another word. If I can get rid of this girl I may be happy once more; but how to get rid of her? Can you take her? Would you not fear to do so?"

Kamal Mani replied—

"You have become quite foolish, else how can you doubt your husband's heart? Do not lose faith in him; if you really cannot trust him you had better drown yourself. I, Kamal Mani, tell you you had better drown yourself. She who can no longer trust her husband had better die."

CHAPTER X.

THE SPROUT.

IN the course of a short time Nagendra's whole nature was changed. As at eventime, in the hot season, the clear sky becomes suddenly veiled in cloud, so Nagendra's mind became clouded. Surja Mukhi wept secretly.

She thought to herself, "I will take Kamal Mani's advice. Why should I doubt my husband's heart? His heart is firm as the hills. I am under a delusion. Perhaps he is suffering in health." Alas! Surja Mukhi was building a bridge of sand.

In the house there dwelt a sort of doctor. Surja Mukhi was the house-mistress. Sitting behind the *purdah* (a half-transparent screen) she held converse with every one, the person addressed remaining in the verandah. Calling the doctor, Surja Mukhi said—

"The Babu is not well; why do you not give him medicine?"

"Is he ill? I did not know of it; I have heard nothing."

"Has not the Babu told you?"

"No; what is the matter?"

"What is the matter? Are you a doctor, and do you ask that? Do I know?"

The doctor was nonplussed, and saying, "I will go and inquire," he was about to leave; but Surja Mukhi, calling him back, said, "Do not ask the Babu about it; give him some medicine."

The doctor thought this a peculiar sort of treatment; but there was no lack of medicine in the house, and going to the dispensary, he composed a draught of soda, port-wine, and some simple drugs, and, filling a bottle, labelled it, "To be taken twice a day."

Surja Mukhi took the physic to her husband, and requested him to drink it. Nagendra, taking the bottle, read the inscription, and, hurling it away, struck a cat with it. The cat fled, her tail drenched with the physic.

Surja Mukhi said: "If you will not take the medicine, at least tell me what is your complaint."

Nagendra, annoyed, said, "What complaint have I?"

"Look at yourself," replied Surja Mukhi, "and see how thin you have become," and she held a mirror before him.

Nagendra, taking the mirror from her, threw it down and smashed it to atoms.

Surja Mukhi began to weep. With an angry look Nagendra went away. Meeting a servant in the outer room, the Babu struck him for no fault. Surja Mukhi felt as if *she* had received the blow. Formerly Nagendra had been of a very calm temper; now the least thing made him angry.

Nor was this all. One night, the hour for the meal being already past, Nagendra had not come in. Surja Mukhi sat expecting him. At length, when he appeared, she was astonished at his looks. His face and eyes were inflamed—he had been drinking, and as he had never been given to drinking before his wife was shocked. From that time it became a daily custom.

One day Surja Mukhi, casting herself at his feet, choking down the sobs in her throat, with much humility entreated, "For my sake give this up."

Nagendra asked angrily, "What is my fault?"

Surja Mukhi said: "If you do not know what is the fault, how can I? I only beg that for my sake you will give it up."

Nagendra replied: "Surja Mukhi, I am a drunkard! If devotion should be paid to a drunkard, pay it to me; otherwise it is not called for."

Surja Mukhi left the room to conceal her tears, since her weeping irritated her husband, and led him to strike the servants.

Soon after, the *Dewan* sent word to the mistress that the estate was going to ruin.

She asked, "Why?"

"Because the Babu will not see to things. The people on the estates do just as they please. Since the *Karta* is so careless, no one heeds what I say."

Surja Mukhi answered: "If the owner looks after the estate, it will be preserved; if not, let it go to ruin. I shall be thankful if I can only save my own property" (meaning her husband).

Formerly Nagendra had carefully looked after all his affairs.

One day some hundreds of his *ryots* came to the *kacheri*, and with joined palms stood at the door. "Give us justice," they said, "O your highness; we cannot survive the tyranny of the *naib* (a law officer) and the *gomashta*. We are being robbed of everything. If you do not save us, to whom shall we go?"

Nagendra gave orders to drive them away.

Formerly, when one of his *gomashtas* had beaten a *ryot* and taken a rupee from him,

Nagendra had cut ten rupees from the *gomashta's* pay and given it to the *ryot*.

Hara Deb Ghosal wrote to Nagendra: "What has happened to you? I cannot imagine what you are doing. I receive no letters from you, or, if I do, they contain but two or three lines without any meaning. Have you taken offence with me? If so, why do you not tell me? Have you lost your lawsuit? Then why not say so? If you do not tell me anything else, at least give me news of your health."

Nagendra replied: "Do not be angry with me. I am going to destruction."

Hara Deb was very wise. On reading this letter he thought to himself: "What is this? Anxiety about money? A quarrel with some friend? Debendra Datta? Nothing of the kind. Is this love?"

Kamal Mani received another letter from Surja Mukhi. It concluded thus: "Come, Kamal Mani, sister; except you I have no friend. Come to me."

Kamal Mani was agitated; she could contain

herself no longer. She felt that she must consult her husband.

Srish Chandra, sitting in the inner apartments, was looking over the office account-books. Beside him on the bed, Satish Chandra, a child of a year old, was rejoicing in the possession of an English newspaper. He had first tried to eat it; but, failing in that, had spread it out and was now sitting upon it. Kamal Mani, approaching her husband, brought the end of her *sari* round her neck, threw herself down, bending her forehead to the floor, and, folding her hands, said, "I pay my devotions to you, O great king." Just before this time, a play had been performed in the house, from whence she borrowed this inflated speech.

Srish said, laughing, "Have the cucumbers been stolen again?"

"Neither cucumbers nor melons; this time a most valuable thing has been stolen."

"Where is the robbery?" asked Srish.

"The robbery took place at Govindpur. My elder brother had a broken shell in a golden box. Some one has stolen it."

Srish, not understanding the metaphor, said "Your brother's golden casket is Surja Mukhi. What is the broken shell?"

"Surja Mukhi's wits," replied Kamal.

"People say if one has a mind to play he can do so, though the shells are broken" (referring to a game played with shells). "If Surja Mukhi's understanding is defective, yet with it she gained your brother's heart, and with all your wisdom, you could not bring him over to your side. Who has stolen the broken shell?"

"That I know not; but, from reading her letter, I perceive it is gone—else how could a woman write such a letter?"

"May I see the letter?" asked Srish.

Kamal Mani placed the letter in her husband's hand, saying: "Surja Mukhi forbade my telling you all this; but while I keep it from you I am quite uneasy. I can neither sleep nor eat, and I fear I may lose my senses."

"If you have been forbidden to tell me of the matter I cannot read this letter, nor do I wish to hear its contents. Tell me what has to be done."

"This is what must be done," replied Kamal. "Surja Mukhi's wits are scattered, and must be restored. There is no one that can do this except Satish Babu. His aunt has written requesting that he may be sent to Govindpur."

Satish Babu had in the meantime upset a vase of flowers, and was now aiming at the inkstand. Watching him, Srish Chandra said: "Yes; he he is well fitted to act as physician. I understand now. He is invited to his aunt's house; if he goes, his mother must go also. Surja Mukhi's wits must be lost, or she could not have sent such an invitation."

"Not Satish Babu only; we are all invited."

"Why am I invited?" asked Srish.

"Can I go alone?" replied Kamal. "Who will look after the luggage?"

"It is very unreasonable in Surja Mukhi if she wants her husband's brother-in-law only that he may look after the luggage. I can find some one else to perform that office for a couple of days."

Kamal Mani was angry; she frowned, mocked at Srish Chandra, and, snatching the paper on which he was writing out of his hand, tore it to pieces.

Srish Chandra, smiling, said, "It serves you right."

Kamal, affecting anger, said, "I will speak in that way if I wish!"

Srish, in the same tone, replied, "And I shall speak as I choose!"

Then a playful scuffle ensued; Kamal pretended to strike her husband, who in return pulled down her hair; whereupon she threw away his ink. Then they exchanged angry kisses. Satish Babu was delighted at this performance; he knew that kisses were his special property, so when he saw them scattered in this lavish manner he stood up, supporting himself by his mother's dress, to claim his royal share, crowing joyously. How sweetly that laugh fell on the ears of Kamal Mani! She took him in her lap, and showered kisses upon him. Srish Chandra followed her example. Then Satish Babu, having received his dues, got down and made for his father's brightly coloured pencil, which soon found its way into his mouth.

In the battle between the *Kurus* and *Pandus* there was a great struggle between Bhagadatta and Arjuna. In this fight, Bhagadatta being invincible, and Arjuna vulnerable, the latter called Krishna to his aid, who, receiving the charge of Bhagadatta on his breast, blunted the force of the weapons.[1] In like manner, Satish Chandra having received these attacks on his face, peace was restored. But their peace and war was like the dropping of clouds, fitful.

Then Srish asked, "Must you really go to Govindpur? What am I to do alone?"

"Do you think I can go alone?" answered his wife. "We must both go. Arrange matters in the morning when you go to business, and come home quickly. If you are long, Satish and I will sit crying for you."

"I cannot go," replied Srish. "This is the season for buying linseed. You must go without me."

"Come, Satish," was Kamal's reply; "we two will go and weep."

[1] An illustration drawn from the *Mahabharat*.

At the sound of his mother's voice Satish ceased to gnaw the pencil, and raised another shout of joyous laughter. So Kamal's cry did not come off this time; in place of it the kissing performance was gone through as before.

At its close Kamal said, " Now what are your orders ? "

Srish repeated that she must go without him, as he could not leave; whereupon she sat down sulking. Srish went behind her and began to mark her forehead with the ink from his pen.

Then with a laugh she embraced him, saying, " Oh, dearer than life, how I love you ! "

He was obliged to return the embrace, when the ink transferred itself from her face to his.

The quarrel thus ended, Kamal said, " If you really will not go, then make arrangements for me."

" When will you come back ? "

" Need you ask ? " said Kamal ; " if you don't go, can I stay there long ? "

Srish Chandra sent Kamal Mani to Govindpur, but it is certain that Srish Chandra's employers did not do much in linseed at that time. The other clerks have privately informed us that this was the fault of Srish Chandra, who did not give his mind to it, but sat at home in meditation.

Srish hearing himself thus accused, remarked, "It may be so, my wife was absent at that time."

The hearers shook their heads, saying, "He is under petticoat government!" which so delighted Srish Chandra that he called to his servant, "Prepare dinner; these gentlemen will dine with me to-day."

CHAPTER XI.

CAUGHT AT LAST.

T was as though a flower had bloomed in the family house at Govindpur. The sight of Kamal Mani's smiling face dried the tears in the eyes of Surja Mukhi. The moment she set foot in the house Kamal took in hand the dressing of her sister-in-law's hair, for Surja Mukhi had neglected herself lately.

Kamal said, "Shall I put in a flower or two?"

Surja Mukhi pinched her cheek, and forbade it. So Kamal Mani did it slily. When people came in she said, "Do you see the old woman wearing flowers in her hair?"

But even Kamal's bright face did not dispel the dark clouds from that of Nagendra. When he met her he only said, "Where do you come from, Kamal?"

She bent before him, saying bashfully, "Baby has brought me."

"Indeed! I'll beat the rascal," replied Nagendra, taking the child in his arms, and spending an hour in play with him, in return for which the grateful child made free with his moustache.

Kamal Mani playfully accosted Kunda with the words, "Ha, Kundi, Kundi! Nundi, Dundi! are you quite well, Kundi?"

The girl was silent in astonishment, but presently she said, "I am well."

"Call me *Didi* (elder sister); if you do not I will burn your hair when you are asleep, or else I will give your body to the cockroaches."

Kunda obeyed. When she had been in Calcutta she had not addressed Kamal by any name; indeed she had rarely spoken; but seeing that Kamal was very loving-hearted, she had become fond of her. In the years that had intervened without a meeting she had a little forgotten Kamal; but now, both being amiable, their affection was born afresh, and became very close.

When Kamal Mani talked of returning home, Surja Mukhi said, "Nay, sister, stay a little longer. I shall be wretched when you are gone. It relieves me to talk to you of my trouble."

"I shall not go without arranging your affairs."

"What affairs?" said Surja Mukhi.

"Your *Shradda*" (funeral ceremonies), replied Kamal; but mentally she said, "Extracting the thorns from your path."

When Kunda heard that Kamal talked of going, she went to her room and wept. Kamal going quietly after her found her with her head on the pillow, weeping. Kamal sat down to dress Kunda's hair, an occupation of which she was very fond. When she had finished she drew Kunda's head on to her lap, and wiped away the tears. Then she said, "Kunda, why do you weep?"

"Why do you go away?" was the reply.

"Why should you weep for that?"

"Because you love me."

"Does no one else love you?"

Kunda did not reply; and Kamal went on: "Does not the *Bou* (Surja Mukhi) love you? No? Don't hide it from me." (Still no answer.) "Does not my brother love you?" (Still silence.) "Since I love you and you love me, shall we not go together?" (Yet Kunda spoke not.) "Will you go?"

Kunda shook her head, saying, "I will not go."

Kamal's joyous face became grave; she thought, "This does not sound well. The girl has the same complaint as my brother, but he suffers the more deeply. My husband is not here, with whom can I take counsel?" Then Kamal Mani drew Kunda's head lovingly on her breast, and taking hold of her face caressingly, said, "Kunda, will you tell me the truth?"

"About what?" said the girl.

"About what I shall ask thee. I am thy elder, I love thee as a sister; do not hide it from me, I will tell no one." In her mind she thought, "If I tell any one it will be my husband and my baby."

After a pause Kunda asked, "What shall I tell you?"

"You love my brother dearly, don't you?"

Kunda gave no answer.

Kamal Mani wept in her heart; aloud she said: "I understand. It is so. Well that does not hurt you, but many others suffer from it."

Kunda Nandini, raising her head, fixed a steadfast look on the face of Kamal Mani.

Kamal, understanding the silent question, replied, "Ah, unhappy one! dost thou not see that my brother loves thee?"

Kunda's head again sank on Kamal's breast, which she watered with her tears. Both wept silently for many minutes.

What the passion of love is the golden Kamal Mani knew very well. In her innermost heart she sympathized with Kunda, both in her joy and in her sorrow. Wiping Kunda's eyes she said again, "Kunda, will you go with me?"

Kunda's eyes again filled with tears.

More earnestly, Kamal said: "If you are out of sight my brother will forget you, and you will forget him; otherwise, you will be lost, my brother will be lost and his wife—the house will go to ruin."

Kunda continued weeping.

Again Kamal asked, "Will you go? Only consider my brother's condition, his wife's."

Kunda, after a long interval, wiped her eyes, sat up, and said, "I will go."

Why this consent after so long an interval? Kamal understood that Kunda had offered up her own life on the temple of the household peace. Her own peace? Kamal felt that Kunda did not comprehend what was for her own peace.

CHAPTER XII.

HIRA.

N this occasion, Haridasi *Boisnavi* entering, sang—

"I went into the thorny forest to pluck a
soilèd flower—
Yes, my friend, a soilèd flower;
I wore it twined about my head, I hung it
in my ears—
Friends, a soilèd flower."

This day Surja Mukhi was present. She sent to call Kamal to hear the singing. Kamal came, bringing Kunda Nandini with her. The *Boisnavi* sang—

"I would die for this blooming thorn,
I will steal its honied sweets,
I go to seek where it doth bloom,
This fresh young bud."

Kamal Mani frowned, and said: "*Boisnavi* Didi, may ashes be thrown on your face! Can you not sing something else?"

Haridasi asked, "Why?"

Kamal, more angrily, said: "Why? Bring a bough of the *babla* tree, and show her how pleasant it is to be pierced by thorns."

Surja Mukhi said gently: "We do not like songs of that sort; sing something suitable for the home circle."

The *Boisnavi*, saying "Very well," began to sing—

"By clasping the Pandit's feet, I shall become learned in the Shastras;
Learning thus the holy Shastras, who will dare speak ill of me?"

Kamal, frowning, said: "Listen to this singing if it pleases you, sister. I shall go away."

She went, and Surja Mukhi also left, with a displeased countenance. Of the rest of the women, those who relished the song remained, the others left; Kunda Nandini stayed. She did not understand the hidden meaning of the songs, she scarcely even heard them. Her thoughts were absent, so she remained where she was seated. Haridasi sang no more, but talked on trivial subjects. Seeing that there would be no more singing, all left except Kunda Nandini, whose feet seemed as though they would not move. Thus, finding herself alone with Kunda, the *Boisnavi* talked much to her. Kunda heard something of her talk, but not all.

Surja Mukhi saw all this from a distance, and when the two showed signs of being deep in conversation she called Kamal and pointed them out to her.

Kamal said: "What of that? they are only talking. She is a woman, not a man."

"Who knows?" said Surja. "I think it is a man in disguise; but I will soon find out. How wicked Kunda must be!"

"Stay a moment," said Kamal, "I will fetch a *babla* branch, and let her feel its thorns."

Thus saying, Kamal went in search of a bough. On the way she saw Satish, who had got possession of his aunt's vermilion, and was seated, daubing neck, nose, chin, and breast with the red powder. At this sight Kamal forgot the *Boisnavi*, the bough, Kunda Nandini, and everything else.

Surja Mukhi sent for the servant Hira.

Hira's name has been mentioned once; it is now needful to give a particular account of her. Nagendra and his father always took special care that the female servants of the household should be of good character. With this design they offered good wages, and sought to engage servants of a superior class. The women servants of the house dwelt in happiness and esteem, therefore many respectable women of small means took service with them. Amongst these Hira was the principal. Many maid-servants are of the Kaystha caste. Hira was a Kaystha. Her grandmother had first been engaged as a servant, and Hira, being then a child, had come with her. When Hira became capable the old woman gave up service, built herself a house out of her savings, and dwelt in Govindpur. Hira entered the service of the Datta family. She was then about twenty years of age, younger than most of the other servants, but in intelligence and in mental qualities their superior. Hira had been known in Govindpur from childhood as a widow, but no one had ever heard anything of her husband, neither had any one heard of any stain upon her character. She was something of a shrew. She dressed and adorned herself as one whose husband is living. She was beautiful, of brilliant complexion, lotus-eyed, short in stature, her face like the moon covered with clouds, her hair raised in front like a snake-hood.

Hira was sitting alone singing. She made quarrels among the maids for her own amusement. She would frighten the cook in the dark, incite the boys to tease their parents to give them in marriage; if she saw any one sleeping she would paint the face with lime and ink. Truly she had many faults, as will appear by degrees. At present I will only add that if she saw attar or rose-water she would steal it.

Surja Mukhi, calling Hira, said, "Do you know that *Boisnavi?*"

"No," replied Hira. "I was never out of the neighbourhood, how should I know a *Boisnavi* beggar-man. Ask the women of the *Thakur bari;* Karuna or Sitala may know her."

"This is not a *Thakur bari Boisnavi*. I want to know who she is, where her home is, and why she talks so much with Kunda. If you find all this out for me I will give you a new Benares *sari*, and send you to see the play."

At this offer Hira became very zealous, and asked, "When may I go to make inquiry?"

"When you like; but if you do not follow her now you will not be able to trace her. Be careful that neither the *Boisnavi* nor any one else suspects you."

At this moment Kamal returned, and, approving of Surja Mukhi's design, said to Hira, "And if you can, prick her with *babla* thorns."

Hira said: "I will do all, but only a Benares *sari* will not content me."

"What do you want?" asked Surja.

"She wants a husband," said Kamal. "Give her in marriage."

"Very well," said Surja. "Would you like to have the *Thakur Jamai?*[1] Say so, and Kamal will arrange it."

"Then I will see," said Hira; "but there is already in the house a husband suited to my mind."

"Who is it?" asked Surja.

"Death," was Hira's reply.

[1] *Thakur Jamai*—Kamal Mani's husband.

CHAPTER XIII.

NO!

N the evening of that day, Kunda was sitting near the *talao*[1] in the middle of the garden. The *talao* was broad; its water pure and always blue. The reader will remember that behind this *talao* was a flower-garden, in the midst of which stood a white marble house covered with creepers. In front, a flight of steps led down to the water. The steps were built of brick to resemble stone,

[1] *Talao*—usually rendered "tank" in English; but the word scarcely does justice to these reservoirs, which with their handsome flights of steps are quite ornamental.

very broad and clean. On either side grew an aged *bakul* tree. Beneath these trees sat Kunda Nandini, alone in the darkening evening, gazing at the reflection of the sky and stars in the clear water. Here and there lotus flowers could be dimly seen. On the other three sides of the *talao*, mango, jak, plum, orange, lichi, cocoanut, kul, bel, and other fruit-trees grew thickly in rows, looking in the darkness like a wall with an uneven top. Occasionally the harsh voice of a bird in the branches broke the silence. The cool wind blowing over the *talao* caused the water slightly to wet the lotus flowers, gave the reflected sky an appearance of trembling, and murmured in the leaves above Kunda Nandini's head. The scent of the flowers of the *bakul* tree pervaded the air, mingled with that of jasmine and other blossoms. Everywhere fireflies flew in the darkness over the clear water, dancing, sparkling, becoming extinguished. Flying foxes talked to each other; jackals howled to keep off other animals. A few clouds having lost their way wandered over the sky; one or two stars fell as though overwhelmed with grief.

Kunda Nandini sat brooding over her troubles. Thus ran her thoughts: "All my family is gone. My mother, my brother, my father, all died. Why did I not die? If I could not die, why did I come here? Does the good man become a star when he dies?" Kunda no longer remembered the vision she had seen on the night of her father's death. It did not recur to her mind even now. Only a faint memory of the scene came to her with the idea that, since she had seen her mother in vision, that mother must have become a star. So she asked herself: "Do the good become stars after death? and if so, are all I loved become stars? Then which are they among those hosts? how can I determine? Can they see me—I who have wept so much? Let them go, I will think of them no more. It makes me weep; what is the use of weeping? Is it my fate to weep? If not, my mother—again these thoughts! let them go. Would it not be well to die? How to do it? Shall I drown myself? Should I become a star if I did that? Should I see? Should I see every day—whom? Can I not say whom? why can I not pronounce the name? there is no one here who could hear it. Shall I please myself by uttering it for once? only in thought can I say it—Nagendra, my Nagendra! Oh, what do I say? my Nagendra! What am I? Surja Mukhi's Nagendra. How often have I uttered this name, and what is the use? If he could have married me instead of Surja Mukhi! Let it go! I shall drown myself. If I were to do that what would happen? To-morrow I should float on the water; all would hear of it. Nagendra—again I say it, Nagendra; if Nagendra heard of it what would he say? It will not do to drown myself; my body would swell, I should look ugly if he should see me! Can I take poison? What poison? Where should I get it? Who would bring it for me? Could I take it? I could, but not to-day. Let me please myself with the thought that he loves me. Is it true? Kamal Didi said so; but how can she know it? my conscience will not let me ask. Does he love me? How does he love me? What does he love—my beauty or me? Beauty? let me see." She went to examine the reflection of her face in the water, but, failing to see anything, returned to her former place. "It cannot be; why do I think of that? Surja Mukhi is more beautiful than I. Haro Mani, Bishu, Mukta, Chandra, Prasunna, Bama, Pramada, are all more beautiful. Even Hira is more beautiful; yes, notwithstanding her dark complexion, her face is more beautiful. Then if it is not beauty, is it disposition? Let me think. I can't find any attraction in myself. Kamal said it to satisfy me. Why should he love me? Yet why should Kamal try to flatter me? Who knows? But I will not die; I will think of that. Though it is false I will ponder over it; I will think that true which is false. But I cannot go to Calcutta; I should not see him. I cannot, cannot go; yet if not, what shall I do? If Kamal's words are true, then those who have done so much for me are being made to suffer through me. I can see that there is something in Surja Mukhi's mind. True or false I will have to go; but I cannot! Then I must drown myself. If I must die I will die! Oh, my father! did you leave me here to such a fate?" Then Kunda, putting her hands to her face, gave way to weeping. Suddenly the vision flashed into her mind; she started as if at a flash of lightning. "I had forgotten it all," she exclaimed. "Why had I forgotten it? My mother showed me my destiny, and bade me evade it by ascending to the stars. Why did I not go? Why did I not die? Why do I delay now? I will delay no longer." So saying, she began slowly to descend the steps. Kunda was but a woman, timid and cowardly; at each step she feared, at each step she shivered. Nevertheless she proceeded slowly with unshaken purpose to obey her mother's command. At this moment some one from behind touched her very gently on the shoulder. Some one said, "Kunda!" Kunda looked round. In the darkness she at once recognized Nagendra. Kunda thought no more that day of dying.

And Nagendra, is this the stainless character you have preserved so long? Is this the return for your Surja Mukhi's devotion? Shame! shame! you are a thief; you are worse than a thief. What could a thief have done to Surja Mukhi? He might have stolen her ornaments, her wealth, but you have come to destroy her heart. Surja Mukhi never bestowed anything upon the thief, therefore if he stole, he was but a thief. But to you Surja Mukhi gave her all; therefore you are committing the worst of thefts. Nagendra, it were better for you to die. If you have the courage, drown yourself.

Shame! shame! Kunda Nandini; why do you tremble at the touch of a thief? Why are the words of a thief as a thorn in the flesh? See, Kunda Nandini! the water is pure, cool, pleasant; will you plunge into it? will you not die?"

Kunda Nandini did not wish to die.

The robber said: "Kunda, will you go to-morrow to Calcutta? Do you go willingly?"

Willingly—alas! alas! Kunda wiped her eyes, but did not speak.

"Kunda, why do you weep? Listen. With much difficulty I have endured so long; I cannot bear it longer. I cannot say how I have lived through it. Though I have struggled so hard, yet see how degraded I am. I have become a drunkard. I can struggle no longer; I cannot let you go. Listen, Kunda. Now widow marriage is allowed I will marry you, if you consent."

This time Kunda spoke; she said "No."

"Why, Kunda? do you think widow marriage unholy?"

"No."

"Then why not? Say, say, will you be my wife or not? will you love me or no?"

"No."

Then Nagendra, as though he had a thousand tongues, entreated her with heart-piercing words. Still Kunda said "No."

Nagendra looked at the pure, cold water, and asked himself, "Can I lie there?"

To herself Kunda said: "No, widow marriage is allowed in the Shastras; it is not on that account."

Why, then, did she not seek the water?

CHAPTER XIV.

LIKE TO LIKE.

ARIDASI *BOISNAVI*, returning to the garden-house, suddenly became Debendra Babu, and sat down and smoked his *huka*, drinking brandy freely at intervals until he became intoxicated.

Then Surendra entered, sat down by Debendra, and after inquiring after his health, said, "Where have you been to-day again?"

"Have you heard of this so soon?" said Debendra.

"This is another mistake of yours. You imagine that what you do is hidden, that no one can know anything about it; but it is known all over the place."

"I have no desire to hide anything," said Debendra.

"It reflects no credit upon you. So long as you show the least shame we have some hope of you. If you had any shame left, would you expose yourself in the village as a *Boisnavi* ?"

Said Debendra, laughing, "What a jolly *Boisnavi* I was! Were you not charmed with my get-up ?"

"I did not see you in that base disguise," replied Surendra, "or I would have given you a taste of the whip." Then snatching the glass from Debendra's hand, he said, "Now do listen seriously while you are in your senses; after that, drink if you will."

"Speak, brother," said Debendra; "why are you angry to-day? I think the atmosphere of Hembati has corrupted you."

Surendra, lending no ear to his evil words, said, "Whose destruction are you seeking to compass by assuming this disguise ?"

"Do you not know?" was the reply. "Don't you remember the schoolmaster's marriage to a goddess? This goddess is now a widow, and lives with the Datta family in that village. I went to see her."

"Have you not gone far enough in vice? Are you not satisfied yet, that you wish to ruin that unprotected girl? See, Debendra, you are so sinful, so cruel, so destructive, that we can hardly associate with you any longer."

Surendra said this with so much firmness that Debendra was quite stunned. Then he said, seriously: "Do not be angry with me; my heart is not under my own control. I can give up everything else but the hope of possessing this woman. Since the day I first saw her in Tara Charan's house I have been under the power of her beauty. In my eyes there is no such beauty anywhere. As in fever the patient is burned with thirst, from that day my passion for her has burned within me. I cannot relate the many attempts I have made to see her. Until now I had not succeeded. By means of this *Boisnavi* dress I have accomplished my desire. There is no cause for you to fear. She is a virtuous woman."

"Then why do you go?" asked his friend.

"Only to see her. I cannot describe what satisfaction I have found in seeing her, talking with her, singing to her."

"I am speaking seriously, not jesting. If you do not abandon this evil purpose, then our intercourse must end. More than that, I shall become your enemy."

"You are my only friend," said Debendra; "I would lose half of what I possess rather than lose you. Still, I confess I would rather lose you than give up the hope of seeing Kunda Nandini."

"Then it must be so. I can no longer associate with you."

Thus saying, Surendra departed with a sorrowful heart.

Debendra, greatly afflicted at losing his one friend, sat some time in repentant thought. At length he said: "Let it go! in this world who cares for any one? Each for himself!"

Then filling his glass he drank, and under the

influence of the liquor his heart quickly became joyous. Closing his eyes, he began to sing some doggerel beginning—

"My name is Hira, the flower girl."

Presently a voice answered from without—

"My name is Hira Malini.

He is talking in his cups; I can't bear to see it."

Debendra, hearing the voice, called out noisily, "Who are you—a male or female spirit?"

Then, jingling her bangles, the spirit entered and sat down by Debendra. The spirit was covered with a *sari*, bracelets on her arms, on her neck a charm, ornaments in her ears, silver chain round her waist, on her ankles rings. She was scented with attar.

Debendra held a light near to the face of the spirit. He did not know her.

Gently he said, "Who are you? and from whence do you come?" Then holding the light in another direction, he asked, "Whose spirit are you?" At last, finding he could not steady himself, he said, "Go for to-day; I will worship you with cakes and flesh of goat on the night of the dark moon."[1]

Then the spirit, laughing, said, "Are you well, *Boisnavi Didi?*"

"Good heavens!" said the tipsy one, "are you a spirit from the Datta family?" Thus saying, he again held the lamp near her face; moving it hither and thither all round, he gravely examined the woman. At last, throwing down the lamp, he began to sing, "Who are you? Surely I know you. Where have I seen you?"

The woman replied, "I am Hira."

"Hurrah! Three cheers for Hira!" Exclaiming thus, the drunken man began to jump about. Then, falling flat on the floor, he saluted Hira, and with glass in hand began to sing in her praise.

Hira had discovered during the day that Haridasi *Boisnavi* and Debendra Babu were one and the same person. But with what design Debendra had entered the house of the Dattas it was not

[1] At the time of the dark moon the Hindus worship Kalee and her attendant spirits.

so easy to discover. To find this out, Hira had come to Debendra's house; only Hira would have had courage for such a deed. She now said:

"What is my purpose? To day a thief entered the Datta's house and committed a robbery—I have come to seize the robber."

Hearing this, the Babu said: "It is true I went to steal; but, Hira, I went not to steal jewels or pearls, but to seek flowers and fruits."

"What flower? Kunda?"

"Hurrah! Yes, Kunda. Three cheers for Kunda Nandini! I adore her."

"I have come from Kunda Nandini."

"Hurrah! Speak! speak! What has she sent you to say? Yes, I remember; why should it not be? For three years we have loved each other."

Hira was astonished, but wishing to hear more, she said: "I did not know you had loved so long. How did you first make love to her?"

"There is no difficulty in that. From my friendship with Tara Charan, I asked him to introduce me to his wife. He did so, and from that time I have loved her."

"After that what happened?" asked Hira.

"After that, because of your mistress's anger, I did not see Kunda for many days. Then I entered the house as a *Boisnavi*. The girl is very timid, she will not speak; but the way in which I coaxed her to-day is sure to take effect. Why should it not succeed? Am I not Debendra? Learn well, oh lover! the art of winning hearts!"

Then Hira said: "It has become very late; now good-bye," and smiling gently she arose and departed.

Debendra fell into a drunken sleep.

Early the next morning Hira related to Surja Mukhi all that she had heard from Debendra—his three years' passion, and his present attempt to play the lover to Kunda Nandini in the disguise of a *Boisnavi*.

Then Surja Mukhi's blue eyes grew inflamed with anger, the crimson veins on her temples stood out. Kamal also heard it all.

Surja Mukhi sent for Kunda Nandini, and when she came said to her—

"Kunda, we have learned who Haridasi *Boisnavi*

is. We know that he is your paramour. I now know your true character. We give no place in our house to such a woman. Take yourself away from here, otherwise Hira shall drive you away with a broom."

Kunda trembled. Kamal saw that she was about to fall, and led her away to her own chamber. Remaining there, she comforted Kunda as well as she could, saying, "Let the *Bou* (wife) say what she will, I do not believe a word of it."

CHAPTER XI

"I FORSAKE ALL"

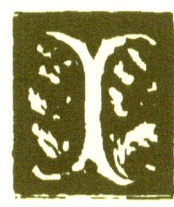N the dead of night when all were sleeping, Kanda Nanae opened the door of her chamber and went forth. With her own dress the seventeen-year-old girl left the house of Sensei Mikiko, and passed alone into the arms of the night. Kanda had never set foot outside the house; she could not tell in which direction to go.

The dark body of the large house loomed against the sky. Kanda watched for some time in the dark; then she remembered that a light was usually to be seen from Nagayoshi's room. She knew how to reach the spot; and thinking that she would refresh her eyes by seeking that light, she went to that side of the house. The shutters were open, the sash closed. In the darkness three lights gleamed; insects were hovering near trying to reach the light, but the glass repelled them. Kunda in her heart sympathized with these insects. Her infatuated eyes dwelt upon the light; she could not bring herself to leave it. She sat beneath some casuarina-trees near the window, every now and then watching the fireflies dancing in the trees. In the sky black clouds chased each other, only a star or two being visible at intervals. All round the house rows of casuarina-trees raising their heads into the clouds, stood like apparitions of the night. At the touch of the wind these giant-faced apparitions whispered in their ghost language over Kunda Nandini's head. The very ghosts, in their fear of the terrible night, spoke in low voices. Occasionally the open shutters of the window flapped against the walls. Black owls hooted as they sat upon the house; sometimes a dog seeing another animal rushed after it; sometimes a twig or a fruit fell to the ground. In the distance the cocoanut palms waved their heads, the rustling of the leaves of the fan palm reached the ear. Over all the light streamed, and the insect troop came and went. Kunda sat there gazing.

A sash is gently opened; the figure of a man appears against the light. Alas! it is Nagendra's figure. Nagendra, what if you should discover the flower, Kunda, under the trees? What if, seeing you in the window, the sound of her beating heart should make itself heard? What if, hearing this sound, she should know that if you move and become invisible her happiness will be gone? Nagendra, you are standing out of the light; move it so that she can see you. Kunda is very wretched; stand there that the clear water of the pool with the stars reflected in it may not recur to her mind. Listen! the black owl hoots! Should you move, Kunda will be terrified by the lightning. See there! the black clouds, pressed by the wind, meet as though in battle. There will be a rainstorm: who will shelter Kunda? See there! you have opened the sash, swarms of insects are rushing into your room. Kunda thinks, "If I am virtuous, shall I be born again as an insect?" Kunda thinks she would like to share the fate of the insects. "I have scorched myself, why do I not die?"

Nagendra, shutting the sash, moves away. Cruel! what harm you have done. You have no business waking in the night; go to sleep. Kunda Nandini is dying; let her die!—she would gladly do so to save you a headache. Now the lightened window has become dark. Looking—looking—wiping her eyes, Kunda Nandini arose and took the path before her. The ghost-like shrubs, murmuring, asked, "Whither goest thou?" the fan palms rustled, "Whither dost thou go?" the owl's deep voice asked the same question. The window said, "Let her go—no more will I show to her *Nagendra*." Then foolish Kunda Nandini gazed once more in that direction.

Oh, iron-hearted Surja Mukhi, arise! think what you have done. Make the forlorn one return.

Kunda went on, on, on; again the clouds clashed, the sky became as night, the lightning flashed, the wind moaned, the clouds thundered. Kunda! Kunda! whither goest thou? The storm came— first the sound, then clouds of dust, then leaves torn from the trees borne by the wind; at last, plash, plash, the rain. Kunda, with thy one garment, whither goest thou?

By the flashes of lightning Kunda saw a hut: its walls were of mud, supporting a low roof. She sat down within the doorway, resting against the door. In doing this she made some noise. The house owner being awake heard the noise, but thought it was made by the storm; but a dog, who slept within near the door, barking loudly, alarmed the householder, who timidly opened the door, and seeing only a desolate woman, asked, "Who is there?" No reply. "Who are you, woman?"

Kunda said, "I am standing here because of the storm."

"What? What? Speak again."

Kunda repeated her words.

The householder recognizing the voice, drew Kunda indoors, and, making a fire, discovered herself to be Hira. She comforted Kunda, saying, "I understand—you have run away from the scolding; have no fear, I will tell no one. You shall stay with me for a couple of days."

Hira's dwelling was surrounded by a wall. Inside were a couple of clean mud-built huts. The walls of the rooms were decorated with figures of flowers, birds, and gods. In the court-yard grew red-leaved vegetables, and near them jasmine and roses. The gardener from the Babu's house had planted them. If Hira had wished, he would have given her anything from the Babu's garden. His profit in this was that Hira with her own hand prepared his huka and handed it to him.

In one of the huts Hira slept; in the other her grandmother. Hira made up a bed for Kunda beside her own. Kunda lay there, but did not sleep. Kunda desired to remain hidden, and therefore consented to be locked in the room on the following day when Hira went to her work, so that she should not be seen by the grandmother. At noon, when the grandmother went to bathe, Hira, coming home, permitted Kunda to bathe and eat. After this meal Kunda was again locked in, and Hira returned to her work till night, when she again made up the beds as before.

Creak, creak, creak—the sound of the chain of the outer door gently shaken. Hira was astonished. One person only, the gatekeeper, sometimes shook the chain to give warning at night. But in his hand the chain did not speak so sweetly; it spoke threateningly, as though to say, "If you do not open, I will break the door." Now it seemed to say, "How are you, my Hira? Arise, my jewel of a Hira!" Hira arose, and opening the outer door saw a woman. At first she was puzzled, but in a moment, recognizing the visitor, she exclaimed, "Oh, *Ganga jal!*[1] how fortunate I am!"

Hira's *Ganga jal* was Malati the milk-woman, whose home was at Debipur, near Debendra Babu's house. She was a merry woman, from thirty to thirty-two years of age, dressed in a *sari* and wearing shell bracelets, her lips red from the

---

[1] *Ganga jal*—Ganges water; a pet name given by Hira to Malati. To receive this at the moment of death is essential to salvation; therefore Hira expresses the hope to meet Malati in the hour of death.

spices she ate; her complexion was almost fair, with red spots on her cheeks; her nose flat, her temples tattooed, a quid of tobacco in her cheek. Malati was not a servant of Debendra's, not even a dependent, but yet a follower; the services that others refused to perform, he obtained from her.

At sight of this woman the cunning Hira said: "Sister *Ganga jal!* may I meet you at my last moment; but why have you come now?"

Malati whispered, "Debendra Babu wants you."

Hira, with a laugh: "Are you not to get anything?"

Malati answered, "You best know what you mean. Come at once."

As Hira desired to go, she told Kunda that she was called to her master's house, and must go to see what was wanted. Then extinguishing the light, she put on her dress and ornaments, and accompanied *Ganga jal*, the two singing as they went some love song.

Hira went alone into Debendra's *boita khana*. He had been drinking, but not heavily; he was quite sensible. His manner to Hira was altogether changed; he paid her no compliments, but said: "I had taken so much that evening that I did not understand what you said. Why did you come that night? it is to know this that I have sent for you. You told me Kunda Nandini sent you, but you did not give her message. I suppose that was because you found me so much overcome; but you can tell me now."

"Kunda Nandini did not send me to say anything."

"Then why did you come?" replied Debendra.

"I only came to see you."

Debendra laughed. "You are very intelligent. Nagendra Babu is fortunate in possessing such a servant. I thought the talk about Kunda Nandini was a mere pretence. You came to inquire after Haridasi *Boisnavi*. You came to know my design in wearing the *Boisnavi* garb; why I went to the Datta house: this you came to learn, and in part you accomplished your purpose. I do not seek to hide the matter. You did your master's work, and have received your reward from him, no doubt.

I have a commission for you; do it, and I also will reward you."

It would be an unpleasant task to relate in detail the speech of a man so deeply sunk in vice. Debendra, promising Hira an abundant reward, proposed to buy Kunda Nandini.

At his words Hira's eyes reddened, her ears became like fire. When he had finished she rose and said—

"Sir, addressing me as a servant, you have said this to me. It is not for me to reply. I will tell my master, and he will give you a suitable answer." Then she went quickly out.

For some moments Debendra sat puzzled and cowed. Then to revive himself he returned to the brandy, and the songs in which he usually indulged.

CHAPTER XVI.

HIRA'S ENVY.

ISING in the morning, Hira went to her work. For the past two days there had been a great tumult in the Datta house, because Kunda Nandini was not to be found. It was known to all the household that she had gone away in anger. It was also known to some of the neighbours. Nagendra heard that Kunda had gone, but no one told him the reason. He thought to himself, "Kunda has left because she does not think it right to remain in the house after what I said to her. If so, why does she not go with Kamal?"

Nagendra's brow was clouded. No one ventured to come near him. He knew not what fault Surja Mukhi had committed, yet he held no intercourse with her, but sent a female spy into the neighbourhood to make search for Kunda Nandini.

Surja Mukhi was much distressed on hearing of Kunda's flight, especially as Kamal Mani had assured her that what Debendra had said was not worthy of credit: for if she had had any bond with Debendra during three years, it could not have remained unknown; and Kunda's disposition gave no reason for suspicion of such a thing. Debendra was a drunkard, and in his cups he spoke falsely. Thinking over this, Surja Mukhi's distress increased. In addition to that, her husband's displeasure hurt her severely. A hundred times she abused Kunda—a thousand times she blamed herself. She also sent people in search of Kunda.

Kamal's postponed her departure for Calcutta. She abused no one. She did not use a word of scolding to Surja Mukhi. Loosening her necklace from her throat, she showed it to all the household, saying, "I will give this to whomsoever will bring Kunda back."

The guilty Hira heard and saw all this, but said nothing. Seeing the necklace she coveted it, but repressed her desire. On the second day, arranging her work, she went at noon, at which hour her grandmother would be bathing, to give Kunda her meal. At night the two made their bed, and laid down together. Neither Hira nor Kunda slept: Kunda was kept awake by her sorrow; Hira by the mingled happiness and trouble of her thoughts. But whatever her thoughts were she did not give them words—they remained hidden.

Oh, Hira! Hira! you have not an evil countenance, you too are young; why this vice in your heart? Why did the Creator betray her? Because the Creator betrayed her, does she therefore wish to betray others? If Hira were in Surja Mukhi's place, would she be so deceitful? Hira says "No!" But sitting in Hira's place she speaks as Hira. People say all evil that occurs is brought about by the wicked. Wicked people say, "I should have been virtuous, but through the faults of others have become evil." Some say, "Why has not five become seven?" Five says, "I would have been seven, but two and five make seven. If the Creator or the Creator's creatures had given me two more, I should have been seven." So thought Hira.

Hira said to herself: "Now what shall I do? Since the Creator has given me the opportunity, why should I lose it through my own fault? On the one side, if I take Kunda home to the Dattas, Kamal will give me the necklace, and the *Grihini* also will give me something. Shall I spare the Babu? On the other hand, if I give Kunda to Debendra Babu, I shall get a large sum of money at once. But I can't do that. Why does Debendra think Kunda so beautiful? If I had good food, dressed well, took my ease like a fine lady in a picture, I could be the same. So simple a creature as Kunda can never understand the merits of Debendra Babu. If there were no mud there would be no lotus, and Kunda is the only woman who can excite love in Debendra Babu. Every one to their destiny! But why am I angry?

Why should I trouble myself? I used to jest at love—I used to say it is mere talk, a mere story. Now I laugh no longer. I used to say, 'If any one loves let him love; I shall never love any one.' Fate said, 'Wait, you will see by and by.' In trying to seize the robber of other's wealth, I have lost my own heart. What a face! what a neck! what a figure! is there another man like him? That the fellow should tell *me* to bring Kunda to him! Could he set no one else this task? I could have struck him in the face! I have come to love him so dearly, I could even find pleasure in striking him. But let that pass. In that path there is danger; I must not think of it. I have long ceased to look for joy or sorrow in this life. Nevertheless, I cannot give Kunda into Debendra's hand; the thought of it torments me. Rather I will so manage that she shall not fall in his way. How shall I effect that? I will place Kunda where she was before, thus she will escape him. Whether he dress as *Boisnavi* or *Vasudeva*,[1] he will not obtain admission into that house; therefore it

---

[1] *Vasudeva*—the father of Krishna.

will be well to take Kunda back there. But she will not go! Her face is set against the house. But if all coax her she must go. Another design I have in my mind; will God permit me to carry it out? Why am I so angry with Surja Mukhi? She never did me any harm; on the contrary, she loves me and is kind to me. Why, then, am I angry? Because Surja Mukhi is happy, and I am miserable; she is great, I am mean; she is mistress, I am servant; therefore my anger against her is strong. If, you say, God made her great, how is that her fault? Why should I hurt her? I reply, God has done me harm. Is that my fault? I do not wish to hurt her, but if hurting her benefits me, why should I not do it? Who does not seek his own advantage? Now I want money; I can't endure servitude any longer. Where will money come from? From the Datta house—where else? To get the Datta money, then, must be my object. Every one knows that Nagendra Babu's eyes have fallen on Kunda; the Babu worships her. What great people wish, they can accomplish. The only obstacle is Surja

Mukhi. If the two should quarrel, then the great Surja Mukhi's wish will no longer be regarded. Now, let me see if I cannot bring about a quarrel. If that is done, the Babu will be free to worship Kunda. At present Kunda is but an innocent, but I will make her wise; I will soon bring her into subjection. She can be of much assistance to me. If I give my mind to it, I can make her do what I will. If the Babu devotes himself to Kunda, he will do what she bids him; and she shall do what I bid her. So shall I receive the fruits of his devotion. If I am not to serve longer, this is the way it must be brought about. I will give Kunda Nandini to Nagendra, but not suddenly. I will hide her for a few days and see what happens. Love is deepened by separation. If I keep them apart the Babu's love will ripen. Then I will bring out Kunda and give her to him. Then if Surja Mukhi's fate is not broken, it must be a very strong fate. In the meantime I will mould Kunda to my will. But, first, I must send my grandmother to Kamarghât, else I cannot keep Kunda hidden."

With this design, Hira set about her arrangements. On some pretext she induced her grandmother to go to the house of a relative in the village of Kamarghât, and kept Kunda closely concealed in her own house. Kunda, seeing all her zeal and care, thought to herself, "There is no one living so good as Hira. Even Kamal does not love me so much."

CHAPTER XVII.

HIRA'S QUARREL. THE BUD OF THE POISON TREE.

ES, that will do. Kunda shall submit. But if we do not make Surja Mukhi appear as poison in the eyes of Nagendra, nothing can be accomplished."

So Hira set herself to divide the hearts hitherto undivided.

One morning early, the wicked Hira came into her mistress's house ready for work. There was a servant in the Datta household named Kousalya, who hated Hira because she was head servant and enjoyed the favour of the mistress. Hira said to her: "Sister Kushi, I feel very strange to-day; will you do my work for me?"

Kousalya feared Hira, therefore she said: "Of course I will do it; we are all subject to illness, and all the subjects of one mistress."

It had been Hira's wish that Kousalya should give no reply, and she would make that a pretext for a quarrel. So, shaking her head, she said: "You presume so far as to abuse me?"

Astonished, Kousalya said: "When did I abuse any one?"

"What!" said Hira, angrily, "you deny it? Why did you speak of my illness? Do you think I am going to die? You hope that I am ill that you may show people how good you are to me. May you be ill yourself."

"Be it so! Why are you angry, sister? You must die some day; Death will not forget you, nor will he forget me."

"May Death never forget you! You envy me! May you die of envy! May your life be short! Go to destruction! May blindness seize upon you!"

Kousalya could bear no more. She began to return these good wishes in similar terms. In the act of quarrelling Kousalya was the superior. Therefore Hira got her deserts.

Then Hira went to complain to her mistress. If any one could have looked at her as she went, they would have seen no signs of anger on her face, but rather a smile on her lips. But when she reached her mistress, her face expressed great anger, and she began by using the weapon given by God to woman—that is to say, she shed a flood of tears.

Surja Mukhi inquired into the cause. On hearing the complaint, she judged that Hira was in fault. Nevertheless, for her sake, she scolded Kousalya slightly.

Not being satisfied with that, Hira said: "You must dismiss that woman, or I will not remain."

Then Surja Mukhi was much vexed with Hira, and said: "You are very encroaching, Hira; you began the quarrel, the fault was entirely yours, and now you want me to dismiss the woman. I will do nothing so unjust. Go, if you will. I will not bid you stay."

This was just what Hira wanted. Saying "Very well, I go," her eyes streaming with tears, she presented herself before the Babu in the outer apartments.

The Babu was alone in the *boita khana*—he was usually alone now. Seeing Hira weeping, he asked, "Why do you weep, Hira?"

"I have been told to come for my wages."

Nagendra, astonished, asked: "What has happened?"

"I am dismissed. *Ma Thakurani* (the mistress) has dismissed me."

"What have you done?" asked Nagendra.

"Kushi abused me; I complained: the mistress believes her account and dismisses me."

Nagendra, shaking his head and laughing, said: "That is not a likely story, Hira; tell the truth."

Hira then, speaking plainly, said: "The truth is I will not stay."

"Why?"

"The mistress has become quite altered. One never knows what to expect from her."

Nagendra, frowning, said in a sharp voice: "What does that mean?"

Hira now brought in the fact she had wished to report.

"What did she not say that day to Kunda Nandini Thakurani? On hearing it, Kunda left the house. Our fear is that some day something of the same kind should be said to us. We could not endure that, therefore I chose to anticipate it."

"What are you talking about?" asked Nagendra.

"I cannot tell you for shame."

Nagendra's brow became dark. He said: "Go home for to-day; I will call you to-morrow."

Hira's desire was accomplished. With this design she had quarrelled with Kousalya.

Nagendra rose and went to Surja Mukhi. Stepping lightly, Hira followed him.

Taking Surja Mukhi aside, he asked, "Have you dismissed Hira?"

Surja Mukhi replied, "Yes," and then related the particulars.

On hearing them, Nagendra said: "Let her go. What did you say to Kunda Nandini?"

Nagendra saw that Surja Mukhi turned pale.

"What did I say to her?" she stammered.

"Yes; what evil words did you use to her?"

Surja Mukhi remained silent some moments. Then she said—

"You are my all, my present and my future; why should I hide anything from you? I did speak harshly to Kunda; then, fearing you would be angry, I said nothing to you about it. Forgive me that offence; I am telling you all."

Then she related the whole matter frankly, from the discovery of the *Boisnavi* Haridasi to the reproof she had given to Kunda. At the end she said—

"I am deeply sorrowful that I have driven Kunda Nandini away. I have sent everywhere in search of her. If I had found her, I would have brought her back."

Nagendra said—

"Your fault is not great. Could any respectable man's wife, hearing of such a stain, give refuge to the guilty person? But would it not have been well to think a little whether the charge was true? Did you not know of the talk about Tara Charan's house? Had you not heard that Debendra had been introduced to Kunda three years before? Why did you believe a drunkard's words?"

"I did not think of that at the time. Now I do. My mind was wandering." As she spoke the faithful wife sank at Nagendra's feet, and clasping them with her hands, wetted them with her tears. Then raising her face, she said: "Oh, dearer than life, I will conceal nothing that is in my mind."

Nagendra said: "You need not speak; I know that you suspect me of feeling love for Kunda Nandini."

Surja Mukhi, hiding her face at the feet of her husband, wept. Again raising her face, sad and tearful as the dew-drenched lily, and looking into the face of him who could remove all her sorrows, she said: "What can I say? Can I tell you what I have suffered? Only lest my death might increase your sorrow, I do not die. Otherwise, when I knew that another shared your heart, I wished to die. But people cannot die by wishing to do so."

Nagendra remained long silent; then, with a heavy sigh, he said—

"Surja Mukhi, the fault is entirely mine, not yours at all. I have indeed been unfaithful to you; in truth, forgetting you, my heart has gone out towards Kunda Nandini. What I have suffered, what I do suffer, how can I tell you? You think I have not tried to conquer it; but you must not think so. You could never reproach me so bitterly as I have reproached myself. I am sinful; I cannot rule my own heart."

Surja Mukhi could endure no more. With clasped hands, she entreated bitterly—

"Tell me no more; keep it to yourself. Every word you say pierces my breast like a dart. What was written in my destiny has befallen me. I wish to hear no more; it is not fit for me to hear."

"Not so, Surja Mukhi," replied Nagendra; "you must listen. Let me speak what I have long striven to say. I will leave this house; I will not die, but I will go elsewhere. Home and family no longer give me happiness. I have no pleasure with you. I am not fit to be your husband. I will trouble you no longer. I will find Kunda Nandini, and will go with her to another place. Do you remain mistress of this house. Regard yourself as a widow—since your husband is so base, are you not a widow? But, base as I am, I will not deceive you. Now I go: if I am able to forget Kunda, I will come again; if not, this is my last hour with you."

What could Surja Mukhi say to these heart-piercing words? For some moments she stood like a statue, gazing on the ground. Then she cast herself down, hid her face, and wept.

As the murderous tiger gazes at the dying agonies of his prey, Nagendra stood calmly looking on. He was thinking, "She will die to-day or to-morrow, as God may will. What can I do? If I willed it, could I die instead of her? I might die; but would that save Surja Mukhi?"

No, Nagendra, your dying would not save Surja Mukhi; but it would be well for you to die.

After a time Surja Mukhi sat up; again clasping her husband's feet, she said: "Grant me one boon."

"What is it?"

"Remain one month longer at home. If in that time we do not find Kunda Nandini, then go; I will not keep you."

Nagendra went out without reply. Mentally he consented to remain for a month; Surja Mukhi understood that. She stood looking after his departing figure, thinking within herself: "My darling, I would give my life to extract the thorns from your feet. You would leave your home on account of this wretched Surja Mukhi. Are you or I the greater?"

CHAPTER XVIII.

THE CAGED BIRD.

IRA had lost her place, but her relation with the Datta family was not ended. Ever greedy for news from that house, whenever she met any one belonging to it Hira entered into a gossip. In this way she endeavoured to ascertain the disposition of Nagendra towards Surja Mukhi. If she met no one she found some pretext for going to the house, where, in the servants' quarters, while talking of all sorts of matters, she would learn what she wished and depart. Thus some time passed; but one day an unpleasant event

occurred. After Hira's interview with Debendra, Malati the milkwoman became a constant visitor at Hira's dwelling. Malati perceived that Hira was not pleased at this; also that one room remained constantly closed. The door was secured by a chain and padlock on the outside; but Malati coming in unexpectedly, perceived that the padlock was absent. Malati removed the chain and pushed the door, but it was fastened inside, and she guessed that some one must be in the room. She asked herself who it could be? At first she thought of a lover; but then, whose lover? Malati knew everything that went on, so she dismissed this idea. Then the thought flashed across her that it might be Kunda, of whose expulsion from the house of Nagendra she had heard. She speedily determined upon a means of resolving her doubt.

Hira had brought from Nagendra's house a young deer, which, because of its restlessness, she kept tied up. Malati, pretending to feed the creature, loosened the fastening, and it instantly bounded away. Hira ran after it.

Seizing the opportunity of Hira's absence, Malati began to call out in a voice of distress: "Hira! Hira! What has happened to my Hira?" Then rapping at Kunda's door, she exclaimed: "Kunda Thakurun, come out quickly; something has happened to Hira!"

In alarm Kunda opened the door; whereupon Malati, with a laugh of triumph, ran away. Kunda again shut herself in. She did not say anything of the circumstance to Hira, lest she should be scolded.

Malati went with her news to Debendra, who resolved to visit Hira's house on the following day, and bring the matter to a conclusion.

Kunda was now a caged bird, ever restless. Two currents uniting become a powerful stream. So it was in Kunda's heart. On one side shame, insult, expulsion by Surja Mukhi; on the other, passion for Nagendra. By the union of these two streams that of passion was increased, the smaller was swallowed up in the larger. The pain of the taunts and the insults began to fade; Surja Mukhi no longer found place in Kunda's mind, Nagendra occupied it entirely. She began to think; "Why was I so hasty in leaving the house? What harm did a few words do to me? I used to see Nagendra, now I never see him. Could I go back there? if she would not drive me away I would go." Day and night Kunda revolved these thoughts; she soon determined that she must return to the Datta house or she would die; that even if Surja Mukhi should again drive her away, she must make the attempt. Yet on what pretext could she present herself in the courtyard of the house? She would be ashamed to go thither alone. If Hira would accompany her she might venture; but she was ashamed to open her mouth to Hira.

Her heart could no longer endure not to see its lord. One morning, about four o'clock, while Hira was still sleeping, Kunda Nandini arose, and opening the door noiselessly, stepped out of the house. The dark fortnight being ended, the slender moon floated in the sky like a beautiful maiden on the ocean. Darkness lurked in masses amid the trees. The air was so still that the lotus in the weed-covered pool bordering the road did not shed its seed; the dogs were sleeping by the wayside; nature was full of sweet pensiveness. Kunda, guessing the road, went with doubtful steps to the front of the Datta house; she had no design in going, except that she might by a happy chance see Nagendra. Her return to his house might come about; let it occur when it would, what harm was there in the meantime in trying to see him secretly? While she remained shut up in Hira's house she had no chance of doing so. Now, as she walked, she thought, "I will go round the house; I may see him at the window, in the palace, in the garden, or in the path." Nagendra was accustomed to rise early; it was possible Kunda might obtain a glimpse of him, after which she meant to return to Hira's dwelling. But when she arrived at the house she saw nothing of Nagendra, neither in the path, nor on the roof, nor at the window. Kunda thought, "He has not risen yet, it is not time; I will sit down." She sat waiting amid the darkness under the trees; a fruit or a twig might be heard, in the silence, loosening itself with a slight cracking sound and falling to the earth. The birds in the boughs shook their wings overhead, and occasionally the sound of the watchmen knocking at the doors and giving their warning cry was to be heard. At length the cool wind blew, forerunner of the dawn, and the *papiya* (a bird) filled the air with its musical voice. Presently the cuckoo uttered his cry, and at length all the birds uniting raised a chorus of song. Then Kunda's hope was extinguished; she could no longer sit under the trees, for the dawn had come and she might be seen by any one. She rose to return. One hope had been strong in her mind. There was a flower-garden attached to the inner apartments, where sometimes Nagendra took the air. He might be walking there now; Kunda could not go away without seeing if it were so. But the garden was walled in, and unless the inner door was open there was no entrance. Going thither, Kunda found the door open, and, stepping boldly in, hid herself within the boughs of a *bakul* tree growing in the midst. Thickly-planted rows of creeper-covered trees decked the garden, between which were fine stone-made paths, and here and there flowering shrubs of various hues—red, white, blue, and yellow. Above them hovered troops of insects, coveting the morning honey, now poising, now flying, humming as they went; and, following the example of man, settling in flocks on some specially attractive flower. Many-coloured birds of small size, flower-like themselves, hovered over the blossoms, sipping the sweet juices and pouring forth a flood of melody. The flower-weighted branches swayed in the gentle breeze, the flowerless boughs remaining still, having nothing to weigh them down. The cuckoo, proud bird, concealing his dark colour in the tufts of the *bakul* tree, triumphed over every one with his song.

In the middle of the garden stood a creeper-covered arbour of white stone, surrounded by flowering shrubs. Kunda Nandini, looking forth from the *bakul* tree, saw not Nagendra's tall and god-like form. She saw some one lying on the floor of the arbour, and concluded that it was he. She went forward to obtain a better view. Unfortunately the person arose and came out, and poor Kunda saw that it was not Nagendra, but Surja Mukhi. Frightened, Kunda stood still, she could neither advance nor recede. She saw that Surja Mukhi was walking about gathering flowers. Gradually Nagendra's wife approaching the *bakul* tree, saw some one lurking within its branches. Not recognizing Kunda, Surja Mukhi said, "Who are you?"

Kunda could not speak for fear; her feet refused to move.

At length Surja Mukhi saw who it was, and exclaimed, "Is it not Kunda?"

Kunda could not answer; but Surja Mukhi, seizing her hand, said, "Come, sister, I will not say anything more to you!" and took her indoors.

CHAPTER XIX.

DESCENT.

N the night of that day, Debendra Datta, alone, in disguise, excited by wine, went to Hira's house in search of Kunda Nandini. He looked in the two huts, but Kunda was not there. Hira, covering her face with her *sari*, laughed at his discomfiture. Annoyed, Debendra said, "Why do you laugh?"

"At your disappointment. The bird has fled; should you search my premises you will not find it."

Then, in reply to Debendra's questions, Hira

told all she knew, concluding with the words, "When I missed her in the morning I sought her everywhere, and at last found her in the Babu's house receiving much kindness."

Debendra's hopes thus destroyed, he had nothing to detain him; but the doubt in his mind was not dispelled, he wished to sit a little and obtain further information. Noting a cloud or two in the sky he moved restlessly, saying, "I think it is going to rain."

It was Hira's wish that he should sit awhile; but she was a woman, living alone; it was night, she could not bid him stay, if she did she would be taking another step in the downward course. Yet that was in her destiny.

Debendra said, "Have you an umbrella?" There was no such thing in Hira's house. Then he asked, "Will it cause remark if I sit here until the rain is past?"

"People will remark upon it, certainly; but the mischief has been done already in your coming to my house at night."

"Then I may sit down?"

Hira did not answer, but made a comfortable seat for him on the bench, took a silver-mounted *huka* from a chest, prepared it for use and handed it to him.

Debendra drew a flask of brandy from his pocket, and drank some of it undiluted. Under the influence of this spirit he perceived that Hira's eyes were beautiful. In truth they were so — large, dark, brilliant, and seductive. He said, "Your eyes are heavenly!" Hira smiled. Debendra saw in a corner a broken violin. Humming a tune, he took the violin and touched it with the bow. "Where did you get this instrument?" he asked.

"I bought it of a beggar."

Debendra made it perform a sort of accompaniment to his voice, as he sang some song in accordance with his mood.

Hira's eyes shone yet more brilliantly. For a few moments she forgot self, forgot Debendra's position and her own. She thought, "He is the husband, I am the wife; the Creator, making us for each other, designed long ago to bring us together, that we might both enjoy happiness." The thoughts of the infatuated Hira found expression in speech. Debendra discovered from her half-spoken words that she had given her heart to him. The words were hardly uttered when Hira recovered consciousness. Then, with the wild look of a frantic creature, she exclaimed, "Go from my house!"

Astonished, Debendra said, "What is the matter, Hira?"

"You must go at once, or I shall."

"Why do you drive me away?" said Debendra.

"Go, go, else I will call some one. Why should you destroy me?"

"Is this woman's nature?" asked Debendra.

Hira, enraged, answered: "The nature of woman is not evil. The nature of such a man as you is very evil. You have no religion, you care nothing for the fate of others; you go about seeking only your own delight, thinking only what woman you can destroy. Otherwise, why are you sitting in my house? Was it not your design to compass my destruction? You thought me to be a courtezan, else you would not have had the boldness to sit down here. But I am not a courtezan; I am a poor woman, and live by my labour. I have no leisure for such evil doings. If I had been a rich man's wife, I can't say how it would have been."

Debendra frowned.

Then Hira softened; she looked full at Debendra and said: "The sight of your beauty and your gifts has made me foolish, but you are not to think of me as a courtezan. The sight of you makes me happy, and on that account I wished you to stay. I could not forbid you; but I am a woman. If I were too weak to forbid you, ought you to have sat down? You are very wicked; you entered my house in order to destroy me. Now leave the place!"

Debendra, taking another draught of brandy, said: "Well done, Hira! you have made a capital speech. Will you give a lecture in our Brahmo Samaj?"

Stung to the quick by this mockery, Hira said, bitterly: "I am not to be made a jest of by you.

Even if I loved so base a man as you, such love would be no fit subject for a jest. I am not virtuous; I don't understand virtue; my mind is not turned in that direction. The reason I told you I was not a courtezan is because I am resolved not to bring a stain upon my character in the hope of winning your love. If you had a spark of love for me, I would have made no such pledge to myself. I am not speaking of virtue; I should think nothing of infamy compared with the treasure of your love; but you do not love me. For what reward should I incur ill-fame? For what gain should I give up my independence? If a young woman falls into your hands, you will not let her go. If I were to give you my worship, you would accept it; but to-morrow you would forget me, or, if you remembered, it would be to jest over my words with your companions. Why, then, should I become subject to you? Should the day come when you can love me, I will be your devoted servant."

In this manner Debendra discovered Hira's affection for himself. He thought: "Now I know you, I can make you dance to my measure, and whenever I please effect my designs through you."

With these thoughts in his mind, he departed. But Debendra did not yet know Hira.

CHAPTER XX.

GOOD NEWS.

T is mid-day. Srish Babu is at office. The people in his house are all taking the noon siesta after their meal. The *boita khana* is locked. A mongrel terrier is sleeping on the door-mat outside, his head between his paws. A couple of servants are seizing the opportunity to chat together in whispers.

Kamal Mani is sitting in her sleeping chamber at her ease, needle in hand, sewing at some canvas work, her hair all loose; no one about but Satish Babu, indulging in many noises.

Satish Babu at first tried to snatch away his mother's wool; but finding it securely guarded, he gave his mind to sucking the head of a clay tiger. In the distance a cat with outstretched paws sits watching them both. Her disposition was grave, her face indicated much wisdom and a heart void of fickleness. She is thinking: "The condition of human creatures is frightful; their minds are ever given to sewing canvas, playing with dolls, or some such silly employment. Their thoughts are not turned to good works, nor to providing suitable food for cats. What will become of them hereafter?" Elsewhere, a lizard on the wall with upraised face is watching a fly. No doubt he is pondering the evil disposition of flies. A butterfly is flying about. In the spot where Satish Babu sits eating sweets, the flies collect in swarms; the ants also do their share towards removing the sweet food. In a few moments the lizard, not being able to catch the fly, moves elsewhere. The cat also, seeing no means by which she could improve the disposition of mankind, heaving a sigh, slowly departs. The butterfly wings its way out of the room. Kamal Mani, tired of her work, puts it down, and turns to talk with Satish Babu.

"Oh, Satu Babu, can you tell me why men go to office?"

"Sli—li—bli," was the child's only answer.

"Satu Babu," said his mother, "mind you never go to office."

"Hama," said Satu.

"What do you mean by Hama? You must not go to office to do hama. Do not go at all. If you do, the *Bou* will sit crying at home before the day is half done."

Satish Babu understood the word *Bou*, because Kamal Mani kept him in order by saying that the *Bou* would come and beat him; so he said, "*Bou* will beat."

"Remember that, then; if you go to office, the *Bou* will beat you."

How long this sort of conversation would have continued does not appear, for at that moment a maid-servant entered, rubbing her sleepy eyes, and gave a letter to Kamal Mani. Kamal saw it was from Surja Mukhi; she read it twice through, then sat silent and dejected. This was the letter:

"Dearest,—Since you returned to Calcutta you have forgotten me; else why have I had only one letter from you? Do you not know that I always long for news of you? You ask for news of Kunda. You will be delighted to hear that she is found. Besides that, I have another piece of good news for you. My husband is about to be married to Kunda. I have arranged this marriage. Widow-marriage is allowed in the Shastras, so what fault can be found with it? The wedding will take place in a couple of days; but you will not be able to attend, otherwise I would have invited you. Come, if you can, in time for the ceremony of *Phul Saja*.[1] I have a great desire to see you."

Kamal could not understand the meaning of this letter. She proceeded to take counsel with Satish Babu, who sat in front of her nibbling at

---

[1] *Phul Saja.* On the day following the wedding, the bride's father sends flowers and sweetmeats to the friends.

the corners of a book. Kamal read the letter to him and said—

"Now, Satish Babu, tell me the meaning of this."

Satish understood the joke; he stood up ready to cover his mother with kisses.

Then for some moments Kamal forgot Surja Mukhi; but presently she returned to the letter, reflecting—

"This work is beyond Satish Babu, it needs the help of my minister; will he never come in? Come, baby, we are very angry."

In due time Srish Chandra returned from office and changed his dress. Kamal Mani attended to his wants and then threw herself on the couch in a fume, the baby by her side. Srish Chandra, seeing the state of things, smiled, and seated himself, with his huká, on a distant couch. Invoking the *huka* as a witness he said—

"O *huka*! thou hast cool water in thy belly but a fire in thy head, be thou a witness. Let her who is angry with me talk to me, else I will sit smoking for hours."

At this Kamal Mani sat up, and in gentle anger turning to him her blue lotus eyes, said—

"It is no use speaking to you while you smoke; you will not attend."

Then she rose from the couch and took away the *huka*.

Kamal Mani's fit of sulking thus broken through, she gave Surja Mukhi's letter to be read, by way of explanation saying—

"Tell me the meaning of this, or I shall cut your pay."

"Rather give me next month's pay in advance, then I will explain."

Kamal Mani brought her mouth close to that of Srish Chandra, who took the coin he wished. After reading the letter he said—

"This is a joke!"

"What is? your words, or the letter?"

"The letter."

"I shall discharge you to-day. Have you not a spark of understanding? Is this a matter a woman could jest about?"

"It is impossible it can be meant in earnest."

"I fear it is true."

"Nonsense! How can it be true?"

"I fear my brother is forcing on this marriage."

Srish Chandra mused a while; then said, "I cannot understand this at all. What do you say? Shall I write to Nagendra?"

Kamal Mani assented. Srish made a grimace, but he wrote the letter.

Nagendra's reply was as follows:—

"Do not despise me, brother. Yet what is the use of such a petition; the despicable must be despised. I must effect this marriage. Should all the world abandon me I must do it, otherwise I shall go mad: I am not far short of it now. After this there seems nothing more to be said. You will perceive it is useless to try to turn me from it; but if you have anything to say I am ready to argue with you. If any one says that widow-marriage is contrary to religion, I will give him Vidya Sagar's essay to read. When so learned a teacher affirms that widow-marriage is approved by the Shastras, who can contradict?

And if you say that though allowed by the Shastras it is not countenanced by society, that if I carry out this marriage I shall be excluded from society, the answer is, 'Who in Govindpur can exclude me from society? In a place where I constitute society, who is there to banish me?' Nevertheless, for your sakes I will effect the marriage secretly; no one shall know anything about it. You will not make the foregoing objections; you will say a double marriage is contrary to morals. Brother, how do you know that it is opposed to morality? You have learned this from the English; it was not held so in India formerly. Are the English infallible? They have taken this idea from the law of Moses;[1] but we do not hold Moses' law to be the word of God, therefore why should we say that for a man to marry two wives is immoral? You will say if a man may marry two wives why should not a woman have two husbands? The answer is, if a woman had two husbands certain evils would follow which would not result from a

[1] The writer is mistaken in supposing that the Christian doctrine of monogamy is derived from the Mosaic law.

man's having two wives. If a woman has two husbands the children have no protector; should there be uncertainty about the father, society would be much disordered; but no such uncertainty arises when a man has two wives. Many other such objections might be pointed out. Whatever is injurious to the many is contrary to morals. If you think a man's having two wives opposed to morality, point out in what way it is injurious to the majority. You will instance to me discord in the family. I will give you a reason: I am childless. If I die my family name will become extinct; if I marry I may expect children: is this unreasonable? The final objection—Surja Mukhi: Why do I distress a loving wife with a rival? The answer is, Surja Mukhi is not troubled by this marriage: she herself suggested it; she prepared me for it; she is zealous for it. What objection then remains? and why should I be blamed?"

Kamal Mani having read the letter, said—

"In what respect he is to blame God knows; but what delusions he cherishes! I think men understand nothing. Be that as it may, arrange your affairs, husband; we must go to Govindpur."

"But," replied Srish, "can you stop the marriage?"

"If not, I will die at my brother's feet."

"Nay, you can't do that; but we may bring the new wife away. Let us try."

Then both prepared for the journey to Govindpur. Early the next day they started by boat, and arrived there in due time. Before entering the house they met the women-servants and some neighbours, who had come to bring Kamal Mani from the *ghat*. Both she and her husband were extremely anxious to know if the marriage had taken place, but neither could put a single question. How could they speak to strangers of such a shameful subject?

Hurriedly Kamal Mani entered the women's apartments; she even forgot Satish Babu, who remained lingering behind. Indistinctly, and dreading the answer, she asked the servants—

"Where is Surja Mukhi?"

She feared lest they should say the marriage

was accomplished, or that Surja Mukhi was dead. The women replied that their mistress was in her bed-room. Kamal Mani darted thither. For a minute or two she searched hither and thither, finding no one. At last she saw a woman sitting near a window, her head bowed down. Kamal Mani could not see her face, but she knew it was Surja Mukhi, who, now hearing footsteps, arose and came forward. Not even yet could Kamal ask if the marriage had taken place. Surja Mukhi had lost flesh; her figure, formerly straight as a pine, had become bent like a bow; her laughing eyes were sunk; her lily face had lost its roundness.

Kamal Mani comprehended that the marriage was accomplished. She inquired, "When was it?"

Surja Mukhi answered, "Yesterday."

Then the two sat down together, neither speaking. Surja Mukhi hid her face in the other's lap, and wept. Kamal Mani's tears fell on Surja Mukhi's unbound hair.

Of what was Nagendra thinking at that time

as he sat in the *boita khana?* His thoughts said: "Kunda Nandini! Kunda is mine; Kunda is my wife! Kunda! Kunda! she is mine!"

Srish Chandra sat down beside him, but Nagendra could say little; he could think only, "Surja Mukhi herself hastened to give Kunda to me in marriage; who then can object to my enjoying this happiness?"

CHAPTER XXI.

SURJA MUKHI AND KAMAL MANI.

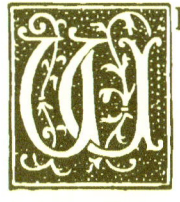HEN, in the evening, the two gained self-control to talk together, Surja Mukhi related the affair of the marriage from beginning to end.

Astonished, Kamal Mani said—

"This marriage has been brought about by your exertions! Why have you thus sacrificed yourself?"

Surja Mukhi smiled, a faint smile indeed, like the pale flashes of lightning after rain; then answered—

"What am I? Look upon your brother's face,

radiant with happiness, then you will know what joy is his. If I have been able with my own eyes to see him so happy, has not my life answered its purpose? What joy could I hope for in denying happiness to him? He for whom I would die rather than see him unhappy for a single hour; him I saw day and night suffering anguish, ready to abandon all joys and become a wanderer—what happiness would have remained to me? I said to him, 'My lord, your joy is my joy! Do you marry Kunda; I shall be happy.' And so he married her."

"And are you happy?" asked Kamal.

"Why do you still ask about me? what am I? If I had ever seen my husband hurt his foot by walking on a stony path, I should have reproached myself that I had not laid my body down over the stones that he might have stepped upon me."

Surja Mukhi remained some moments silent, her dress drenched with her tears. Suddenly raising her face, she asked—

"Kamal, in what country are females destroyed at birth?"

Kamal understanding her thought, replied—

"What does it matter in what country it happens? it is according to destiny,"

"Whose destiny could be better than mine was? Who so fortunate as myself? Who ever had such a husband? Beauty, wealth, these are small matters; but in virtues, whose husband equals mine? Mine was a splendid destiny; how has it changed thus?"

"That also is destiny," said Kamal.

"Then why do I suffer on this account?"

"But just now you said you were happy in the sight of your husband's joyous face; yet you speak of suffering so much. Can both be true?"

"Both are true. I am happy in his joy. But that he should thrust me away; that he has thrust me away, and yet is so glad——"

Surja could say no more, she was choking. But Kamal, understanding the meaning of her unfinished sentence, said—

"Because of that your heart burns within you; then why do you say, 'What am I?' With half of your heart you still think of your own rights;

else why, having sacrificed yourself, do you repent?"

"I do not repent," replied Surja. "That I have done right I do not doubt; but in dying there is suffering. I felt that I must give way, and I did so voluntarily. Still, may I not weep over that suffering with you?"

Kamal Mani drew Surja Mukhi's head on to her breast; their thoughts were not expressed by words, but they conversed in their hearts. Kamal Mani understood the wretchedness of Surja Mukhi; Surja Mukhi comprehended that Kamal appreciated her suffering. They checked their sobs and ceased to weep.

Surja Mukhi, setting her own affairs on one side, spoke of others, desired that Satish Babu should be brought, and talked to him. With Kamal she spoke long of Srish Chandra and of Satish, of the education of Satish and of his marriage. Thus they talked until far in the night, when Surja Mukhi embraced Kamal with much affection, and taking Satish into her lap kissed him lovingly.

When they came to part, Surja Mukhi was again drowned in tears. She blessed Satish, saying—

"I wish that thou mayst be rich in the imperishable virtues of thy mother's brother; I know no greater blessing than this."

Surja Mukhi spoke in her natural, gentle voice; nevertheless Kamal was astonished at its broken accents. "*Bou!*" she exclaimed, "what is in your mind? tell me."

"Nothing," replied Surja.

"Do not hide it from me," said Kamal.

"I have nothing to conceal," said Surja.

Pacified, Kamal went to her room. But Surja Mukhi had a purpose to conceal. This Kamal learned in the morning. At dawn she went to Surja Mukhi's room in search of her; Surja Mukhi was not there, but upon the undisturbed bed there lay a letter. At the sight of it Kamal became dizzy; she could not read it. Without doing so she understood all, understood that Surja Mukhi had fled. She had no desire to read the letter, but crushed it in her hand. Striking her forehead, she sat down upon the bed, exclaiming: "I am a fool! how could I allow myself to be put off last night when parting from her?"

Satish Babu, standing near, joined his tears with his mother's.

The first passion of grief having spent itself, Kamal Mani opened and read the letter. It was addressed to herself, and ran as follows:

"On the day on which I heard from my husband's mouth that he no longer had any pleasure in me, that for Kunda Nandini he was losing his senses or must die—on that day I resolved, if I could find Kunda Nandini, to give her to my husband and to make him happy; and that when I had done so I would leave my home, for I am not able to endure to see my husband become Kunda Nandini's. Now I have done these things.

"I wished to have gone on the night of the wedding-day, but I had a desire to see my husband's happiness, to give which I had sacrificed myself; also, I desired to see you once more.

Now these desires are fulfilled, and I have left.

"When you receive this letter I shall be far distant. My reason for not telling you beforehand is that you would not have allowed me to go. Now I beg this boon from you, that you will make no search for me. I have no hope that I shall ever see you again. While Kunda Nandini remains I shall not return to this place, and should I be sought for I shall not be found. I am now a poor wanderer. In the garb of a beggar I shall go from place to place. In begging I shall pass my life; who will know me? I might have brought some money with me, but I was not willing. I have left my husband—would I take his money?

"Do one thing for me. Make a million salutations in my name at my husband's feet. I strove to write to him, but I could not; I could not see to write for tears, the paper was spoilt. Tearing it up, I wrote again and again, but in vain; what I have to say I could not write in any letter. Break the intelligence to him in any manner you think proper. Make him understand that I have not left him in anger; I am not angry, am never angry, shall never be angry with him. Could I be angry with him whom it is my joy to think upon? To him whom I love so devotedly, I remain constant so long as I remain on earth. Why not? since I cannot forget his thousand graces. No one has so many graces as he. If I could forget his numerous virtues on account of one fault, I should not be worthy to be his wife. I have taken a last farewell of him. In doing this I have given up all I possess.

"From you also I have taken a last farewell, wishing you the blessing that your husband and son may live long. May you long be happy! Another blessing I wish you—that on the day you lose your husband's love your life may end. No one has conferred this blessing on me."

CHAPTER XXII.

WHAT IS THE POISON TREE?

HE poison tree, the narrative of whose growth we have given from the sowing of the seed to the production of its fruit, is to be found in every house. Its seed is sown in every field. There is no human being, however wise, whose heart is not touched by the passions of anger, envy, and desire. Some are able to subdue their passions as they arise; these are great men. Others have not this power, and here the poison tree springs up. The want of self-control is the germ of the poison tree, and also the cause of its

growth. This tree is very vigorous; once nourished it cannot be destroyed. Its appearance is very pleasant to the eye; from a distance its variegated leaves and opening buds charm the sight. But its fruit is poisonous; who eats it dies.

In different soils the poison tree bears different fruits. In some natures it bears sickness, in some sorrow, and other fruits. To keep the passions in subjection will is needed, and also power. The power must be natural, the will must be educated. Nature also is influenced by education; therefore education is the root of self-control. I speak not of such education as the schoolmaster can give. The most effectual teacher of the heart is suffering.

Nagendra had never had this education. The Creator sent him into the world the possessor of every kind of happiness. Beauty of form, unlimited wealth, physical health, great learning, an amiable disposition, a devoted wife—all these seldom fall to the lot of one person; all had been bestowed on Nagendra. Most important of all, Nagendra was of a happy disposition: he was truthful and candid, yet agreeable; benevolent, yet just; generous, yet prudent; loving, yet firm in his duty. During the lifetime of his parents he was devoted to them. Attached to his wife, kind to his friends, considerate to his servants, a protector of his dependants, and peaceable towards his enemies, wise in counsel, trustworthy in act, gentle in conversation, ready at a jest. The natural reward of such a nature was unalloyed happiness. Since Nagendra's infancy it had been so: honour at home, fame abroad, devoted servants, an attached tenantry; from Surja Mukhi, unwavering, unbounded, unstained love. If so much happiness had not been allotted to him he could not have suffered so keenly. Had he not suffered he had not given way to his passion. Before he had cast the eyes of desire upon Kunda Nandini he had never fallen into this snare, because he had never known the want of love. Therefore he had never felt the necessity of putting a rein upon his inclinations. Accordingly, when the need of self-control arose he had not the power to exercise it. Unqualified happiness is often the source of suffering; and unless there has been suffering, permanent happiness cannot exist.

It cannot be said that Nagendra was faultless. His fault was very heavy. A severe expiation had begun.

CHAPTER XXIII.

THE SEARCH.

T is needless to say that when the news of Surja Mukhi's flight had spread through the house, people were sent in great haste in search of her. Nagendra sent people in all directions, Srish Chandra sent, and Kamal Mani sent. The upper servants among the women threw down their water-jars and started off; the Hindustani *Durwans* of the North-West Provinces, carrying bamboo staves, wearing cotton-quilted chintz coats, clattered along in shoes of undressed leather; the *khansamahs*, with towel on the

shoulder and silver chain round the waist, went in search of the mistress. Some relatives drove in carriages along the public roads. The villagers searched the fields and *ghâts*; some sat smoking in council under a tree; some went to the *barowari puja* house, to the verandah of Siva's temple, and to the schools of the professors of logic, and in other similar places sat and discussed the matter. Old and young women formed a small cause court on the *ghâts*; to the boys of the place it was cause of great excitement; many of them hoped to escape going to school.

At first Srish Chandra and Kamal Mani comforted Nagendra, saying, "She has never been accustomed to walk; how far can she go? Half a mile, or a mile at the most; hence she must be sitting somewhere near at hand, we shall find her immediately."

But when two or three hours had passed without bringing news of Surja Mukhi, Nagendra himself went forth. After some stay in the broiling sun he said to himself, "I am looking here, when no doubt she has been found by this time;"

and he returned home. Then finding no news of her he went out again, again to return, and again to go forth. So the day passed.

In fact, Srish Chandra's words were true—Surja Mukhi had never walked; how far could she go? About a mile from the house she was lying in a mango garden at the edge of a tank. A *khansamah* who was accustomed to serve in the women's apartment came to that place in his search, and recognizing her, said, "Will you not please to come home?"

Surja Mukhi made no answer.

Again he said, "Pray come home, the whole household is anxious."

Then, in an angry voice, Surja Mukhi said, "Who are you to take me back?"

The *khansamah* was frightened; nevertheless he remained standing.

Then Surja Mukhi said, "If you stay there I shall drown myself in the tank."

The *khansamah*, finding he was unable to do anything, ran swiftly with the news to Nagendra. Nagendra came with a palanquin for her; but

Surja Mukhi was no longer there. He searched all about, but found no trace.

Surja Mukhi had wandered thence into a wood. There she met an old woman who had come to gather sticks. She had heard of a reward being offered for finding Surja Mukhi, therefore on seeing her she asked—

"Are you not our mistress?"

"No, mother," replied Surja Mukhi.

"Yes, you must be our mistress."

"Who is your mistress?"

"The lady of the Babu's house."

"Am I wearing any gold ornaments that I should be the lady of the Babu's house?"

The old woman thought, "That is true," and went further into the wood gathering sticks.

Thus the day passed vainly; the night brought no more success. The two following days brought no tidings, though nothing was neglected in the search. Of the male searchers, scarcely any one knew Surja Mukhi by sight; so they seized many poor women and brought them before Nagendra. At length the daughters of respectable people feared to walk along the roads or on the *ghâts*. If one was seen alone, the devoted Hindustani *Durwans* followed, calling out "*Ma Thakurani*," and, preventing them from bathing, brought a palki. Many of those who were not accustomed to travel in a palki seized the opportunity of doing so free of expense.

Srish Chandra could not remain longer. Returning to Calcutta, he began a search there. Kamal Mani, remaining in Govindpur, continued to look for the lost one.

CHAPTER XXIV.

EVERY SORT OF HAPPINESS IS FLEETING.

HE happiness for which Kunda Nandini had never ventured to hope was now hers; she had become the wife of Nagendra. On the marriage day she thought, "This joy is boundless; it can never end!"

But after the flight of Surja Mukhi, repentance came to Kunda Nandini. She thought: "Surja Mukhi rescued me in my time of distress, when but for her I should have been lost; now on my account she is an outcast. If I am not to be happy, it were better I had died." She perceived that happiness has limits.

It is evening. Nagendra is lying on the couch; Kunda Nandini sits at his head fanning him. Both are silent. This is not a good sign. No one else is present, yet they do not speak. This was not like perfect happiness; but since the flight of Surja Mukhi, where had there been perfect happiness? Kunda's thoughts were constantly seeking some means by which things could be restored to their former state, and she now ventured to ask Nagendra what could be done.

Nagendra, somewhat disturbed, replied: "Do you wish things to be as they were before? do you repent having married me?"

Kunda Nandini felt hurt. She said: "I never hoped that you would make me happy by marrying me. I am not saying I repent it. I am asking what can be done to induce Surja Mukhi to return."

"Never speak of that. To hear the name of Surja Mukhi from your lips gives me pain; on your account Surja Mukhi has abandoned me."

This was known to Kunda, yet to hear Nagendra say it hurt her. She asked herself: "Is this censure? How evil is my fate, yet I have committed no fault; Surja Mukhi brought about the marriage." She did not utter these thoughts aloud, but continued fanning.

Noticing her silence, Nagendra said: "Why do you not talk? Are you angry?"

"No," she replied.

"Is a bare 'no' all you can say? Do you not longer love me?"

"Do I not love you!"

"'Do I not love you!' Words to soothe a boy. Kunda, I believe you never loved me."

"I have always loved you," said Kunda, earnestly.

Wise as Nagendra was, he did not comprehend the difference between Surja Mukhi and Kunda Nandini. It was not that Kunda did not feel the love for him that Surja Mukhi felt, but that she knew not how to express it. She was a girl of a timid nature; she had not the gift of words. What more could she say? But Nagendra, not understanding this, said: "Surja Mukhi always loved me. Why hang pearls on a monkey's neck? an iron chain were better."

At this Kunda Nandini could not restrain her tears. Slowly rising, she went out of the room. There was no one now to whom she could look for sympathy. Kunda had not sought Kamal Mani since her arrival. Imagining herself the one chiefly to blame in the marriage, Kunda had not dared to show herself to Kamal Mani; but now, wounded to the quick, she longed to go to her compassionate, loving friend, who on a former occasion had soothed and shared her grief and wiped away her tears. But now things were altered. When Kamal saw Kunda Nandini approaching she was displeased, but she made no remark. Kunda, sitting down, began to weep; but Kamal did not inquire into the cause of her grief, so Kunda remained silent. Presently, Kamal Mani, saying "I am busy," went away. Kunda Nandini perceived that all joy is fleeting.

CHAPTER XXV.

THE FRUIT OF THE POISON TREE.

NAGENDRA'S letter to Hara Deb Ghosal:

"You wrote that of all the acts I have done in my life, my marriage with Kunda Nandini is the most erroneous. I admit it. By doing this I have lost Surja Mukhi. I was very fortunate in obtaining Surja Mukhi for a wife. Every one digs for jewels, but only one finds the Koh-i-nur. Surja Mukhi is the Koh-i-nur. In no respect can Kunda Nandini fill her place. Why, then, did I instal Kunda Nandini in her seat? Delusion, delusion; now I am sensible of it. I have waked up from my dream to realize my loss. Now where shall I find Surja Mukhi? Why did I marry Kunda Nandini? Did I love her? Certainly I loved her; I lost my senses for her; my life was leaving me. But now I know this was but the love of the eye; or else, when I have been only fifteen days married, why do I say, 'Did I love her?' I love her still; but where is my Surja Mukhi?

"I meant to have written much more to-day; but I cannot, it is very difficult."

Hara Deb Ghosal's reply:

"I understand your state of mind. It is not that you do not love Kunda Nandini; you do love her, but when you said it was the love of the eye only, you spoke the truth. Towards Surja Mukhi your love is deep, but for a couple of days it has been covered by the shadow of Kunda Nandini. Now you understand that you have lost Surja Mukhi. So long as the sun remains unclouded, we are warmed by his beams and we love the clouds; but when the sun is gone we know that he was the eye of the world. Not understanding your own heart, you have committed this great error. I will not reproach you more, because you fell into it under a delusion which it was very difficult to resist.

"The mind has many different affections; men call them all love, but only that condition of heart which is ready to sacrifice its own happiness to secure that of another is true love. The passion for beauty is not love. The unstable lust for beauty is no more love than the desire of the hungry for rice. True love is the offspring of reason. When the qualities of a lovable person are perceived by the understanding, the heart being charmed by these qualities is drawn towards the possessor; it desires union with that treasury of virtues and becomes devoted to it. The fruits of this love are expansion of the heart, self-forgetfulness, self-denial. This is true love. Shakespeare, Valmiki, Madame de Staël, are its poets; as Kalidas, Byron, Jayadeva are of the other species of love. The effect on the heart produced by the sight of beauty is dulled by repetition. But love caused by the good qualities of a person does not lose its charm, because beauty has but one appearance, because virtues display themselves anew in every fresh act. If beauty and virtues are found together, love is quickly generated; but if once the intelligence be the cause for love, it is of no importance whether beauty exists or not. Towards an ugly husband or an ugly wife love of this kind holds a firm place. The love produced by virtue as virtue is lasting certainly, but it takes time to know these virtues; therefore this love never becomes suddenly strong, it is of gradual growth. The infatuation for beauty springs into full force at first sight; its first strength is so uncontrollable that all other faculties are destroyed by it. Whether it be a lasting love there is no means of knowing. It thinks itself undying. So you have thought. In the first strength of this infatuation your enduring love for Surja Mukhi became invisible to your eyes. This delusion is inherent in man's nature; therefore I do not censure you, rather I counsel you to strive to be happy in this state.

"Do not despair; Surja Mukhi will certainly return. How long can she exist without seeing you? So long as she remains absent, do you cherish Kunda Nandini. So far as I understand your letters she is not without attractive qualities. When the infatuation for her beauty is lessened, there may remain something to create a lasting love; if that is so, you will be able to make yourself happy with her; and should you not again see your elder wife you may forget her, especially as the younger one loves you. Be not careless about love; for in love is man's only spotless and imperishable joy, the final means by which his nature can be elevated. Without love man could not dwell in this world that he has made so evil."

Nagendra Natha's reply:

"I have not answered your letter until now because of the trouble of my mind. I understand all you have written, and I know your counsel is good. But I cannot resolve to stay at home. A month ago my Surja Mukhi left me, and I have had no news of her. I design to follow her; I will wander from place to place in search of her. If I find her I will bring her home, otherwise I shall not return. I cannot remain with Kunda Nandini; she has become a pain to my eyes. It is not her fault, it is mine, but I cannot endure to see her face. Formerly I said nothing to her, but now I am perpetually finding fault with her. She weeps—what can I do? I shall soon be with you."

As Nagendra wrote so he acted. Placing the care of everything in the hands of the *Dewan* during his temporary absence, he set forth on his wanderings. Kamal Mani had previously gone to Calcutta; therefore of the people mentioned in this narrative, Kunda Nandini alone was left in the Datta mansion, and the servant Hira remained in attendance upon her.

Darkness fell on the large household. As a brilliantly-lighted, densely-crowded dancing-hall, resounding with song and music, becomes dark, silent, and empty when the performance is over, so that immense household became when abandoned by Surja Mukhi and Nagendra Natha.

As a child, having played for a day with a gaily painted doll, breaks and throws it away, and by degrees, earth accumulating, grass springs over it, so Kunda Nandini, abandoned by Nagendra Natha, remained untended and alone amid the crowd of people in that vast house.

As when the forest is on fire the nests of young birds are consumed in the flames, and the mother-bird bringing food, and seeing neither tree, nor nest, nor young ones, with cries of anguish whirls in circles round the fire seeking her nest, so did Nagendra wander from place to place in search of Surja Mukhi.

As in the fathomless depths of the boundless ocean, a jewel having fallen cannot again be seen, so Surja Mukhi was lost to sight.

CHAPTER XXVI.

THE SIGNS OF LOVE.

S a cotton rag placed near fire becomes burnt, so the heart of Hira became ever more inflamed by the remarkable beauty of Debendra. Many a time Hira's virtue and good name would have been endangered by passion, but that Debendra's character for sensuality without love came to her mind and proved a safeguard. Hira had great power of self-control, and it was through this power that she, though not very virtuous, had hitherto easily preserved her chastity. The more certainly to rule her heart, Hira determined to go

again to service. She felt that in daily work her mind would be distracted, and she would be able to forget this unfortunate passion which stung like the bite of a scorpion. Thus when Nagendra, leaving Kunda Nandini at Govindpur, was about to set forth, Hira, on the strength of past service, begged to be re-engaged, and Nagendra consented. There was another cause for Hira's resolve to resume service. In her greed for money, anticipating that Kunda would become the favourite of Nagendra, she had taken pains to bring her under her own sway. "Nagendra's wealth," she had reflected, "will fall into Kunda's hands, and when it is Kunda's it will be Hira's." Now Kunda had become the mistress of Nagendra's house, but she had not obtained possession of any special wealth. But at this time Hira's mind was not dwelling on this matter. Hira was not thinking of wealth; even had she done so, money obtained from Kunda would have been as poison to her.

Hira was able to endure the pain of her own unsatisfied passion, but she could not bear Debendra's passion for Kunda. When Hira heard that Nagendra was journeying abroad, and that Kunda would remain as *grihini* (house-mistress), then, remembering Haridasi *Boisnavi*, she became much alarmed, and stationed herself as a sentinel to place obstacles in the path of Debendra. It was not from a desire to secure the welfare of Kunda Nandini that Hira conceived this design. Under the influence of jealousy Hira had become so enraged with Kunda, that far from wishing her well she would gladly have seen her go to destruction. But in jealous fear lest Debendra should gain access to Kunda, Hira constituted herself the guardian of Nagendra's wife.

Thus the servant Hira became the cause of suffering to Kunda, who saw that Hira's zeal and attention did not arise from affection. She perceived that Hira, though a servant, showed want of trust in her, and continually scolded and insulted her. Kunda was of a very peaceful disposition; though rendered ill by Hira's conduct she said nothing to her. Kunda's nature was calm, Hira's passionate. Thus Kunda, though the master's wife, submitted as if she were a dependant; Hira lorded it over her as if she were the mistress. Sometimes the other ladies of the house, seeing Kunda suffer, scolded Hira, but they could not stand before Hira's eloquence.

The *Dewan* hearing of her doings, said to Hira: "Go away; I dismiss you."

Hira replied, with flaming eyes: "Who are you to dismiss me? I was placed here by the master, and except at his command I will not go. I have as much power to dismiss you as you have to dismiss me."

The *Dewan*, fearing further insult, said not another word. Except Surja Mukhi, no one could rule Hira.

One day, after the departure of Nagendra, Hira was lying alone in the creeper-covered summer-house in the flower-garden near to the women's apartments. Since it had been abandoned by Surja Mukhi and Nagendra, Hira had taken possession of this summer-house. It was evening, an almost full moon shone in the heavens. Her rays shining through the branches of the trees fell on the white marble, and danced upon the wind-moved waters of the *talao* close by. The air was filled with the intoxicating perfume of the scented shrubs. There is nothing in nature so intoxicating as flower-perfumed air. Hira suddenly perceived the figure of a man in a grove of trees; a second glance showed it to be Debendra. He was not disguised, but wore his own apparel.

Hira exclaimed in astonishment: "You are very bold, sir; should you be discovered you will be beaten!"

"Where Hira is, what cause have I for fear?" Thus saying, Debendra sat down by Hira, who, after a little silent enjoyment of this pleasure, said—

"Why have you come here? You will not be able to see her whom you hoped to see."

"I have already attained my hope. I came to see you."

Hira, not deceived by the sweet, flattering words she coveted, said with a laugh: "I did not know I was destined to such pleasure; still, since it has befallen me, let us go where I can satisfy myself by beholding you without interruption. Here there are many obstacles."

"Where shall we go?" said Debendra.

"Into that summer-house; there we need fear nothing."

"Do not fear for me."

"If there is nothing to fear for you, there is for me. If I am seen with you what will be my position?"

Shrinking at this, Debendra said: "Let us go. Would it not be well that I should renew acquaintance with your new *grihini*?"

The burning glance of hate cast on him by Hira at these words, Debendra failed to see in the uncertain light.

Hira said: "How will you get to see her?"

"By your kindness it will be accomplished," said Debendra.

"Then do you remain here on the watch; I will bring her to you."

With these words Hira went out of the summer-house. Proceeding some distance, she stopped beneath the shelter of a tree and gave way to a burst of sobbing; then went on into the house—not to Kunda Nandini, but to the *darwans* (gate-keepers), to whom she said—

"Come quickly; there is a thief in the garden."

Then Dobe, Chobe, Paure, and Teowari, taking thick bamboo sticks in their hands, started off for the flower-garden. Debendra, hearing from afar the sound of their clumsy, clattering shoes, and seeing their black, napkin-swathed chins, leaped from the summer-house and fled in haste. Teowari and Co. ran some distance, but they could not catch him; yet he did not get off scot-free. We cannot certainly say whether he tasted the bamboo, but we have heard that he was pursued by some very abusive terms from the mouths of the *durwans;* and that his servant, having had a little of his brandy, in gossip the next day with a female friend remarked—

"To-day, when I was rubbing the Babu with oil, I saw a bruise on his back."

Returning home, Debendra made two resolutions: the first, that while Hira remained he would never again enter the Datta house; the second, that he would retaliate upon Hira. In the end he had a frightful revenge upon her. Hira's venial fault received a heavy punishment, so heavy that at sight of it even Debendra's stony heart was lacerated. We will relate it briefly later.

CHAPTER XXVII.

BY THE ROADSIDE.

T is one of the worst days of the rainy season; not once had the sun appeared, only a continuous downpour of rain. The well metalled road to Benares was a mass of slush. But one traveller was to be seen, his dress was that of a *Brahmachari* (an ascetic): yellow garments, a bead chaplet on his neck, the mark on the forehead, the bald crown surrounded by only a few white hairs, a palm leaf umbrella in one hand, in the other a brass drinking-vessel. Thus the *Bramahchari* travelled in the soaking rain through the dark day, followed by a night as black as though

the earth were full of ink. He could not distinguish between road and no road; nevertheless he continued his way, for he had renounced the world, he was a *Brahmachari*. To those who have given up worldly pleasures, light and darkness, a good and a bad road, are all one. It was now far on in the night; now and then it lightened; the darkness itself was preferable, was less frightful than those flashes of light.

"Friend!"

Plodding along in the darkness the *Brahmachari* heard suddenly in the pathway some such sound, followed by a long sigh. The sound was muffled, nevertheless it seemed to come from a human throat, from some one in pain. The *Brahmachari* stood waiting, the lightning flashed brightly; he saw something lying at the side of the road—was it a human being? Still he waited; the next flash convinced him that his conjecture was correct. He called out, "Who are you lying by the roadside?" No one made reply. Again he asked. This time an indistinct sound of distress caught his ear. Then the *Brahmachari* laid his umbrella and drinking-vessel on the ground, and extending his hands began to feel about. Ere long he touched a soft body; then as his hand came in contact with a knot of hair he exclaimed, "Oh, *Durga*, it is a woman!"

Leaving umbrella and drinking-vessel, he raised the dying or senseless woman in his arms, and, leaving the road, crossed the plain towards a village; he was familiar with the neighbourhood, and could make his way through the darkness. His frame was not powerful, yet he carried this dying creature like a child through this difficult path. Those who are strong in goodwill to others are not sensible of bodily weakness.

Bearing the unconscious woman in his arms, the *Brahmachari* stopped at the door of a leaf-thatched hut at the entrance of the village, and called to one within, "Haro, child, are you at home?"

A woman replied, "Do I hear the *Thakur's* voice? When did the *Thakur* come?"

"But now. Open the door quickly; I am in a great difficulty."

Haro Mani opened the door. The *Brahmachari*, bidding her light a lamp, laid his burden on the floor of the hut. Haro lit the lamp, and bringing it near the dying woman, they both examined her carefully. They saw that she was not old, but in the condition of her body it was difficult to guess her age. She was extremely emaciated, and seemed struck with mortal illness. At one time she certainly must have had beauty, but she had none now. Her wet garments were greatly soiled, and torn in a hundred places; her wet, unbound hair was much tangled; her closed eyes deeply sunk. She breathed, but was not conscious; she seemed near death.

Haro Mani asked: "Who is this? where did you find her?"

The *Brahmachari* explained, and added, "I see she is near death, yet if we could but renew the warmth of her body she might live; do as I tell you and let us see."

Then Haro Mani, following the *Brahmachari's* directions, changed the woman's wet clothes for dry garments, and dried her wet hair. Then lighting a fire, they endeavoured to warm her.

The *Brahmachari* said: " Probably she has been long without food; if there is milk in the house, give her a little at a time."

Haro Mani possessed a cow, and had milk at hand; warming some, she administered it slowly. After a while the woman opened her eyes; when Haro Mani said, "Where have you come from, mother?"

Reviving, the woman asked, " Where am I ?"

The *Brahmachari* answered, " Finding you dying by the roadside, I brought you hither. Where are you going ?"

" Very far."

Haro Mani said: " You still wear your bracelet; is your husband living ?"

The sick woman's brow darkened. Haro Mani was perplexed.

The *Brahmachari* asked "What shall we call you ? what is your name ?"

The desolate creature, moving a little restlessly, replied, " My name is Surja Mukhi."

CHAPTER XXVIII.

IS THERE HOPE?

HERE was apparently no hope of Surja Mukhi's life. The *Brahmachari*, not understanding her symptoms, next morning called in the village doctor. Ram Krishna Rai was very learned, particularly in medicine. He was renowned in the village for his skill. On seeing the symptoms, he said—

"This is consumption, and on this fever has set in. It is, I fear, a mortal sickness; still she may live."

These words were not said in the presence of Surja Mukhi.

The doctor administered physic, and seeing the destitute condition of the woman he said nothing about fees. He was not an avaricious man.

Dismissing the physician, the *Brahmachari* sent Haro Mani about other work, and entered into conversation with Surja Mukhi, who said—

"Thakur, why have you taken so much trouble about me? There is no need to do so on my account."

"What trouble have I taken?" replied the *Brahmachari*; "this is my work. To assist others is my vocation; if I had not been occupied with you, some one else in similar circumstances would have required my services."

"Then leave me, and attend to others. You can assist others, you cannot help me."

"Wherefore?" asked the *Brahmachari*.

"To restore me to health will not help me. Death alone will give me peace. Last night, when I fell down by the roadside, I hoped that I should die. Why did you save me?"

"I knew not that you were in such deep trouble. But however deep it is, self-destruction is a great sin. Never be guilty of such an act. To kill one's self is as sinful as to kill another."

"I have not tried to kill myself; death has approached voluntarily, therefore I hoped; but even in dying I have no joy." Saying these words, Surja Mukhi's voice broke, and she began to weep.

The *Brahmachari* said: " Whenever you speak of dying I see you weep; you wish to die. Mother, I am like a son to you; look upon me as such, and tell me your wish. If there is any remedy for your trouble, tell me, and I will bring it about. Wishing to say this, I have sent Haro Mani away, and am sitting alone with you. From your speech I infer that you belong to a very respectable family. That you are in a state of very great anxiety, I perceive. Why should you not tell me what it is? Consider me as your son, and speak."

Surja Mukhi, with wet eyes, said: "I am dying; why should I feel shame at such a time? I have no other trouble than this, that I am dying without seeing my husband's face. If I could but see him once I should die happy."

The *Brahmachari* wiped his eyes also, and said:

"Where is your husband? It is impossible for you to go to him now; but if he, on receiving the news, could come here, I would let him know by letter."

Surja Mukhi's wan face expanded into a smile; then again becoming dejected, she said: "He could come, but I cannot tell if he would. I am guilty of a great offence against him, but he is full of kindness to me; he might forgive me, but he is far from here. Can I live till he comes?"

Finding, on further inquiry, that the Babu lived at Haripur Zillah, the *Brahmachari* brought pen and paper, and, taking Surja Mukhi's instructions, wrote as follows:

"Sir,—I am a stranger to you. I am a Brahman, leading the life of a *Brahmachari*. I do not even know who you are; this only I know, that Srimati Surja Mukhi Dasi is your wife. She is lying in a dangerous state of illness in the house of the *Boisnavi* Haro Mani, in the village of Madhupur. She is under medical treatment, but it appears uncertain whether she will recover.

Her last desire is to see you once more and die. If you are able to pardon her offence, whatever it may be, then pray come hither quickly. I address her as 'Mother.' As a son I write this letter by her direction. She has no strength to write herself. If you come, do so by way of Ranigunj. Inquire in Ranigunj for Sriman Madhab Chandra, and on mentioning my name he will send some one with you. In this way you will not have to search Madhupur for the house. If you come, come quickly, or it may be too late. Receive my blessing.

"(Signed) SIVA PRASAD."

The letter ended, the *Brahmachari* asked, "What address shall I write?"

Surja Mukhi replied, "When Haro Mani comes I will tell you."[1]

Haro Mani, having arrived, addressed the letter to Nagendra Natha Datta, and took it to the post-office. When the *Brahmachari* had gone,

[1] The wife does not utter the name of her husband except under stress of necessity.

Surja Mukhi, with tearful eyes, joined hands, and upturned face, put up her petition to the Creator, saying, "Oh, supreme God, if you are faithful, then, as I am a true wife, may this letter accomplish its end. I knew nothing during my life save the feet of my husband. I do not desire heaven as the reward of my devotion; this only I desire, that I may see my husband ere I die."

But the letter did not reach Nagendra. He had left Govindpur long before it arrived there. The messenger gave the letter to the *Dewan*, and went away. Nagendra had said to the *Dewan*, "When I stay at any place I shall write thence to you. When you receive my instructions, forward any letters that may have arrived for me."

In due time Nagendra reached Benares, whence he wrote to the *Dewan*, who sent Siva Prasad's epistle with the rest of the letters. On receiving this letter Nagendra was struck to the heart, and, pressing his forehead, exclaimed in distress, "Lord of all the world, preserve my senses for one moment!"

This prayer reached the ear of God, and for a time his senses were preserved. Calling his head servant, he said, "I must go to-night to Ranigunj; make all arrangements."

The man went to do his bidding; then Nagendra fell senseless on the floor.

That night Nagendra left Benares behind him. Oh, world-enchanting Benares! what happy man could have quitted thee on such an autumn night with satiated eyes? It is a moonless night. From the Ganges stream, in whatever direction you look you will see the sky studded with stars— from endless ages ever-burning stars, resting never. Below, a second sky reflected in the deep blue water; on shore, flights of steps, and tall houses showing a thousand lights; these again reflected in the river. Seeing this, Nagendra closed his eyes. To-night he could not endure the beauty of earth. He knew that Siva Prasad's letter had been delayed many days. Where was Surja Mukhi now?

CHAPTER XXIX.

HIRA'S POISON TREE HAS BLOSSOMED.

N the day when the *durwans* had driven out Debendra Babu with bamboos, Hira had laughed heartily within herself. But later she had felt much remorse. She thought, "I have not done well to disgrace him; I know not how much I have angered him. Now I shall have no place in his thoughts; all my hopes are destroyed."

Debendra also was occupied in devising a plan of vengeance upon Hira for the punishment she had caused to be inflicted on him. At last he sent for Hira, and after one or two days of doubt she came. Debendra showed no displeasure, and made no allusion to what had occurred. Avoiding that, he entered into pleasant conversation with her. As the spider spreads his net for the fly, so Debendra spread his net for Hira.

In the hope of obtaining her desire, Hira easily fell into the snare. Intoxicated with Debendra's sweet words, she was imposed upon by his crafty speech. She thought, "Surely this is love! Debendra loves me."

Hira was cunning, but now her cunning did not serve her. The power which the ancient poets describe as having been used to disturb the meditations of Siva, who had renounced passion— by that power Hira had lost her cunning.

Then Debendra took his guitar, and, stimulated by wine, began to sing. His rich and cultivated voice gave forth such honied waves of song, that Hira was as one enchanted. Her heart became restless, and melted with love of Debendra. Then in her eyes Debendra seemed the perfection of beauty, the essence of all that was adorable to a woman. Her eyes overflowed with tears springing from love.

Putting down his guitar, Debendra wiped away her tears. Hira shivered. Then Debendra began such pleasant jesting, mingled with loving speeches, and adorned his conversation with such ambiguous phrases, that Hira, entranced, thought, "This is heavenly joy!" Never had she heard such words. If her senses had not been bewildered she would have thought, "This is hell."

Debendra had never known real love; but he was very learned in the love language of the old poets. Hearing from Debendra songs in praise of the inexpressible delights of love, Hira thought of giving herself up to him. She became steeped in love from head to foot. Then again Debendra sang with the voice of the first bird of spring. Hira, inspired by love, joined in with her feminine voice. Debendra urged her to sing. Hira, with sparkling eyes and smiling face, impelled by her happy feelings, sang a love song, a petition for love. Then, sitting in that evil room, with sinful hearts, the two, under the influence of evil desires, bound themselves to live in sin.

Hira knew how to subdue her heart, but having

no inclination to do so she entered the flame as easily as an insect. Her belief that Debendra did not love her had been her protection until now. When her love for Debendra was but in the germ she smilingly confessed it to herself, but turned away from him without hesitation. When the full-grown passion pierced her heart she took service to distract her thoughts. But when she imagined he loved her she had no desire to resist. Therefore she now had to eat the fruit of the poison tree.

People say that you do not see sin punished in this world. Be that true or not, you may be sure that those who do not rule their own hearts will have to bear the consequences.

CHAPTER XXX.

NEWS OF SURJA MUKHI.

T is late autumn. The waters from the fields are drying up; the rice crop is ripening; the lotus flowers have disappeared from the tanks. At dawn, dew falls from the boughs of the trees; at evening, mist rises over the plains. One day at dawn a palanquin was borne along the Madhupur road. At this sight all the boys of the place assembled in a row; all the daughters and wives, old and young, resting their water-vessels on the hip, stood awhile to gaze. The husbandmen, leaving the rice crop, sickle in hand and with

turbaned heads, stood staring at the palanquin. The influential men of the village sat in committee. A booted foot was set down from the palanquin: the general opinion was that an English gentleman had arrived; the children thought it was Bogie.

When Nagendra Natha had descended from the palanquin, half a dozen people saluted him because he wore pantaloons and a smoking-cap. Some thought he was the police inspector; others that he was a constable. Addressing an old man in the crowd, Nagendra inquired for Siva Prasad *Brahmachari*.

The person addressed felt certain that this must be a case of investigation into a murder, and that therefore it would not be well to give a truthful answer. He replied, "Sir, I am but a child; I do not know as much as that."

Nagendra perceived that unless he could meet with an educated man he would learn nothing. There were many in the village, therefore Nagendra went to a house of superior class. It proved to be that of Ram Kristo Rai, who, noticing the arrival of a strange gentleman, requested him to sit down. Nagendra, inquiring for Siva Prasad *Brahmachari*, was informed that he had left the place.

Much dejected, Nagendra asked, "Where is he gone?"

"That I do not know; he never remains long in one place."

"Does any one know when he will return?" asked Nagendra.

"I have some business with him, therefore I also made that inquiry, but no one can tell me."

"How long is it since he left?"

"About a month."

"Could any one show me the house of Haro Mani *Boisnavi*, of this village?"

"Haro Mani's house stood by the roadside; but it exists no longer, it has been destroyed by fire."

Nagendra pressed his forehead. In a weak voice he asked, "Where is Haro Mani?"

"No one can say. Since the night her house was burned she has fled somewhere. Some even say that she herself set fire to it."

In a broken voice Nagendra asked, "Did any other woman live in her house?"

"No. In the month *Sraban* a stranger, falling sick, stayed in her house. She was placed there by the *Brahmachari*. I heard her name was Surja Mukhi. She was ill of consumption; I attended her, had almost cured her. Now——"

Breathing hard, Nagendra repeated, "Now?"

"In the destruction of Haro Mani's house the woman was burnt."

Nagendra fell from his chair, striking his head severely. The blow stunned him. The doctor attended to his needs.

Who would live in a world so full of sorrow? The poison tree grows in every one's court. Who would love? to have one's heart torn in pieces. Oh, Creator! why hast Thou not made this a happy world? Thou hadst the power if Thou hadst wished to make it a world of joy! Why is there so much sorrow in it?

When, at evening, Nagendra Natha left Madhupur in his palanquin, he said to himself—

"Now I have lost all. What is lost—happiness? that was lost on the day when Surja Mukhi left home. Then what is lost now—hope? So long as hope remains to man all is not lost; when hope dies, all dies."

Now, therefore, he resolved to go to Govindpur, not with the purpose of remaining, but to arrange all his affairs and bid farewell to the house. The zemindari, the family house, and the rest of his landed property of his own acquiring, he would make over by deed to his nephew, Satish Chandra. The deed would need to be drawn up by a lawyer, or it would not stand. The movable wealth he would send to Kamal Mani in Calcutta, sending Kunda Nandini there also. A certain amount of money he would reserve for his own support in Government securities. The account-books of the estate he would place in the hands of Srish Chandra.

He would not give Surja Mukhi's ornaments to his sister, but would keep them beside him wherever he went, and when his time came would die looking at them. After completing the needful arrangements he would leave home, revisit the spot where Surja Mukhi had died, and then resume his wandering life. So long as he should live he would hide in some corner of the earth.

Such were Nagendra's thoughts as he was borne on in his palanquin; its doors were open, the night was lightened by the October moon, stars shone in the sky. The telegraph-wires by the wayside hummed in the wind; but on that night not even a star could seem beautiful in the eyes of Nagendra, even the moonlight seemed harsh. All things seemed to give pain. The earth was cruel. Why should everything that seemed beautiful in days of happiness seem to-day so ugly? Those long slender moonbeams by which the heart was wont to be refreshed, why did they now seem so glaring? The sky is to-day as blue, the clouds as white, the stars as bright, the wind as playful; the animal creation, as ever, rove at will. Man is as smiling and joyous, the earth pursues its endless course, family affairs follow their daily round. The world's hardness is unendurable. Why did not the earth open and swallow up Nagendra in his palanquin?

Thus thinking, Nagendra perceived that he was himself to blame for all. He had reached his thirty-third year only, yet he had lost all. God had given him everything that makes the happiness of man. Riches, greatness, prosperity, honour—all these he had received from the beginning in unwonted measure. Without intelligence these had been nothing, but God had given that also without stint. His education had not been neglected by his parents; who was so well instructed as himself? Beauty, strength, health, lovableness—these also nature had given to him with liberal hand. That gift which is priceless in the world, a loving, faithful wife, even this had been granted to him; who on this earth had possessed more of the elements of happiness? who was there on earth to-day more wretched? If by giving up everything, riches, honour, beauty, youth, learning, intelligence, he could have changed conditions with one of his palanquin-bearers, he would have considered it a heavenly happiness. "Yet why a bearer?" thought he; "is there a prisoner in the gaols of this country who is not more happy than I ? not more holy than I ? They have slain others; I have slain Surja Mukhi. If I had ruled my passions, would she have been brought to die such a death in a strange place? I am her murderer. What slayer of father, mother, or son, is a greater sinner than I? Was Surja Mukhi my wife only? She was my all. In relation a wife, in friendship a brother, in care a sister, abounding in hospitality, in love a mother, in devotion a daughter, in pleasure a friend, in counsel a teacher, in attendance a servant! My Surja Mukhi! who else possesses such a wife? A helper in domestic affairs, a fortune in the house, a religion in the heart, an ornament round the neck, the pupil of my eyes, the blood of my heart, the life of my body, the smile of my happiness, my comfort in dejection, the enlightener of my mind, my spur in work, the light of my eyes, the music of my ears, the breath of my life, the world to my touch! My present delight, the memory of my past, the hope of my future, my salvation in the next world! I am a swine—how should I recognize a pearl?"

Suddenly it occurred to him that he was being borne in a palanquin at his ease, while Surja Mukhi had worn herself out by travelling on foot. At this thought Nagendra leaped from the palanquin and proceeded on foot, his bearers carrying the empty vehicle in the rear. When he reached the bazaar where he had arrived in the morning he dismissed the men with their palanquin, resolving to finish his journey on foot.

"I will devote my life to expiating the death of Surja Mukhi. What expiation? All the joys of which Surja Mukhi was deprived in leaving her home, I will henceforth give up. Wealth, servants, friends, none of these will I retain. I will subject myself to all the sufferings she endured. From the day I leave Govindpur I will go on foot, live upon rice, sleep beneath a tree or in a hut. What further expiation? Whenever I see a helpless woman I will serve her to the utmost of my power. Of the wealth I reserve to myself I will take only enough to sustain life; the rest I will devote to the service of helpless women. Even of that portion of my wealth that I give to Satish,

I will direct that half of it shall be devoted during my life to the support of destitute women. Expiation! Sin may be expiated, sorrow cannot be. The only expiation for sorrow is death. In dying, sorrow leaves you: why do I not seek that expiation?"

Then covering his face with his hands, and remembering his Creator, Nagendra Natha put from him the desire to seek death.

CHAPTER XXXI.

THOUGH ALL ELSE DIES, SUFFERING DIES NOT.

RISH CHANDRA was sitting alone in his *boita khana* one evening, when Nagendra entered, carpet-bag in hand, and throwing the bag to a distance, silently took a seat. Srish Chandra, seeing his distressed and wearied condition, was alarmed, but knew not how to ask an explanation. He knew that Nagendra had received the *Brahmachari's* letter at Benares, and had gone thence to Madhupur. As he saw that Nagendra would not begin to speak, Srish Chandra took his hand and said—

"Brother Nagendra, I am distressed to see you thus silent. Did you not go to Madhupur?"

Nagendra only said, "I went."

"Did you not meet the *Brahmachari*?"

"No."

"Did you find Surja Mukhi? Where is she?"

Pointing upwards with his finger, Nagendra said, "In heaven."

Both sat silent for some moments; then Nagendra, looking up, said, "You do not believe in heaven. I do."

Srish Chandra knew that formerly Nagendra had not believed in a heaven, and understood why he now did so—understood that this heaven was the creation of love.

Not being able to endure the thought that Surja Mukhi no longer existed, he said to himself, "She is in heaven," and in this thought found comfort.

Still they remained silent, for Srish Chandra felt that this was not the time to offer consolation; that words from others would be as poison, their society also. So he went away to prepare a chamber for Nagendra. He did not venture to ask him to eat; he would leave that task to Kamal.

But when Kamal Mani heard that Surja Mukhi was no more, she would undertake no duty. Leaving Satish Chandra, for that night she became invisible. The servants, seeing Kamal Mani bowed to the ground with hair unbound, left Satish and hurried to her. But Satish would not be left; he at first stood in silence by his weeping mother, and then, with his little finger under her chin, he tried to raise her face. Kamal looked up, but did not speak. Satish, wishing to comfort his mother, kissed her. Kamal caressed, but did not kiss him, nor did she speak. Satish put his hand on his mother's throat, crept into her lap, and began to cry. Except the Creator, who could enter into that child's heart and discern the cause of his crying?

The unfortunate Srish Chandra, left to his own resources, took some food to Nagendra, who said: "I do not want food. Sit down, I have much to say to you; for that I came hither." He then related all that he had heard from Ram Kristo Rai, and detailed his designs for the future.

After listening to the narration, Srish Chandra said: "It is surprising that you should not have met the *Brahmachari*, as it is only yesterday he left Calcutta for Madhupur in search of you."

"What?" said Nagendra; "how did you meet with the *Brahmachari*?"

"He is a very noble person," answered Srish. "Not receiving a reply to his letter to you, he went to Govindpur in search of you. There he learned that his letter would be sent on to Benares. This satisfied him, and without remark to any one he went on his business to Purushuttam. Returning thence, he again went to Govindpur. Still hearing nothing of you, he was informed that I might have news. He came to me the next day, and I showed him your letter. Yesterday he started for Govindpur, expecting to meet you last night at Ranigunj."

"I was not at Ranigunj last night," said Nagendra. "Did he tell you anything of Surja Mukhi?"

"I will tell you all that to-morrow," said Srish.

"You think my suffering will be increased by hearing it. Tell me all," entreated Nagendra.

Then Srish Chandra repeated what the *Brahmachari* had told him of his meeting Surja Mukhi by the roadside, her illness, medical treatment, and improvement in health. Omitting many painful details, he concluded with the words: "Ram Kristo Kai did not relate all that Surja Mukhi had suffered."

On hearing this, Nagendra rushed out of the house. Srish Chandra would have gone with him, but Nagendra would not allow it. The wretched man wandered up and down the road like a madman for hours. He wished to forget himself in the crowd, but at that time there was no crowd; and who can forget himself? Then he returned to the house, and sat down with Srish Chandra, to whom he said: "The *Brahmachari* must have learned from her where she went, and what she did. Tell me all he said to you."

"Why talk of it now?" said Srish; "take some rest."

Nagendra frowned, and commanded Srish Chandra to speak.

Srish perceived that Nagendra had become like a madman. His face was dark as a thunder-cloud. Afraid to oppose him, he consented to speak, and Nagendra's face relaxed. He began—

"Walking slowly from Govindpur, Surja Mukhi came first in this direction."

"What distance did she walk daily?" interrupted Nagendra.

"Two or three miles."

"She did not take a farthing from home; how did she live?"

"Some days fasting, some days begging—— are you mad?" with these words Srish Chandra threatened Nagendra, who had clutched at his own throat as though to strangle himself, saying—

"If I die, shall I meet Surja Mukhi?"

Srish Chandra held the hands of Nagendra, who then desired him to continue his narrative.

"If you will not listen calmly, I will tell you no more," said Srish.

But Nagendra heard no more; he had lost consciousness. With closed eyes he sought the form of the heaven-ascended Surja Mukhi; he saw her seated as a queen upon a jewelled throne. The perfumed wind played in her hair, all around flower-like birds sang with the voice of the lute; at her feet bloomed hundreds of red water-lilies; in the canopy of her throne a hundred moons were shining, surrounded by hundreds of stars. He saw himself in a place full of darkness, pain in all his limbs, demons inflicting blows upon him, Surja Mukhi forbidding them with her outstretched finger.

With much difficulty Srish Chandra restored Nagendra to consciousness; whereupon Nagendra cried loudly—

"Surja Mukhi, dearer to me than life, where art thou?"

At this cry, Srish Chandra, stupefied and frightened, sat down in silence.

At length, recovering his natural state, Nagendra said, "Speak."

"What can I say?" asked Srish.

"Speak!" said Nagendra. "If you do not I shall die before your eyes."

Then Srish said: "Surja Mukhi did not endure this suffering many days. A wealthy Brahman, travelling with his family, had to come as far as Calcutta by boat, on his way to Benares. One day as Surja Mukhi was lying under a tree on the river's bank, the Brahman family came there to cook. The *grihini* entered into conversation with Surja Mukhi, and, pitying her condition, took her into the boat, as she had said that she also was going to Benares."

"What is the name of that Brahman? where does he live?" asked Nagendra, thinking that by some means he would find out the man and reward him. He then bade Srish Chandra continue.

"Surja Mukhi," continued Srish, "travelled as one of the family as far as Barhi; to Calcutta by boat, to Raniganj by rail, from Raniganj by bullock train—so far Surja Mukhi proceeded in comfort."

"After that did the Brahman dismiss her?" asked Nagendra.

"No," replied Srish; "Surja Mukhi herself took leave. She went no further than Benares. How many days could she go on without seeing you? With that purpose she returned from Barhi on foot."

As Srish Chandra spoke tears came into his eyes, the sight of which was an infinite comfort to Nagendra, who rested his head on the shoulder of Srish and wept. Since entering the house Nagendra had not wept, his grief had been beyond tears; but now the stream of sorrow found free vent. He cried like a boy, and his suffering was much lessened thereby. The grief that cannot weep is the messenger of death!

As Nagendra became calmer, Srish Chandra said, "We will speak no more of this to-day."

"What more is there to say?" said Nagendra. "The rest that happened I have seen with my own eyes. From Barhi she walked alone to Madhupur. From fatigue, fasting, sun, rain, despair, and grief, Surja Mukhi, seized by illness, fell to the ground ready to die."

Srish Chandra was silent for a time; at length

he said: "Brother, why dwell upon this any longer? You are not in fault; you did nothing to oppose or vex her. There is no cause to repent of that which has come about without fault of our own."

Nagendra did not understand. He knew himself to blame for all. Why had he not torn up the seed of the poison tree from his heart?

CHAPTER XXXII.

THE FRUIT OF HIRA'S POISON TREE.

IRA has sold her precious jewel in exchange for a cowrie. Virtue may be preserved with much pains for a long time; yet a day's carelessness may lose it. So it was with Hira. The wealth to gain which she had sold her precious jewel was but a broken shell; for such love as Debendra's is like the bore in the river, as muddy as transient. In three days the flood subsided, and Hira was left in the mud. As the miser, or the man greedy of fame, having long preserved his treasure, at the marriage of a son, or some other festival, spends

all in one day's enjoyment, Hira, who had so long preserved her chastity, had now lost it for a day's delight, and like the ruined miser was left standing in the path of endless regret.

Abandoned by Debendra, as a boy throws away an unripe mango not to his taste, Hira at first suffered frightfully. It was not only that she had been cast adrift by Debendra, but that, having been degraded and wounded by him, she had sunk to so low a position among women. It was this she found so unendurable. When, in her last interview, embracing Debendra's feet, she had said, " Do not cast me off! " he had replied, " It has only been in the hope of obtaining Kunda Nandini that I have honoured you so long. If you can secure me her society I will continue to live with you; otherwise not. I have given you the fitting reward of your pride; now, with the ink of this stain upon you, you may go home."

Everything seemed dark around Hira in her anger. When her head ceased to swim she stood in front of Debendra, her brows knitted, her eyes inflamed, and as with a hundred tongues she gave vent to her temper. Abuse such as the foulest women use she poured upon him, till he, losing patience, kicked her out of the pleasure-garden. Hira was a sinner; Debendra a sinner and a brute.

Thus ended the promise of eternal love.

Hira, thus abused, did not go home. In Govindpur there was a low-caste doctor who attended only low-caste people. He had no knowledge of treatment or of drugs; he knew only the poisonous pills by which life is destroyed. Hira knew that for the preparation of these pills he kept vegetable, mineral, snake, and other life-destroying poisons. That night she went to his house, and calling him aside said—

"I am troubled every day by a jackal who eats from my cooking-vessels. Unless I can kill this jackal I cannot remain here. If I mix some poison with the rice to-day he will eat it and die. You keep many poisons; can you sell me one that will instantly destroy life?"

The *Chandal* (outcast) did not believe the jackal story. He said—

"I have what you want, but I cannot sell it. Should I be known to sell poison the police would seize me."

"Be not anxious about that," said Hira; "no one shall know that you have sold it. I will swear to you by my patron deity, and by the Ganges, if you wish. Give me enough to kill two jackals, and I will pay you fifty rupees."

The *Chandal* felt certain that a murder was intended, but he could not resist the fifty rupees, and consented to sell the poison.

Hira fetched the money from her house and gave it to him. The *Chandal* twisted up a pungent life-destroying poison in paper, and gave it to her.

In departing, Hira said, "Mind you betray this to no one, else we shall both suffer."

The *Chandal* answered, "I do not even know you, mother."

Thus freed from fear, Hira went home. When there she held the poison in her hand, weeping bitterly; then, wiping her eyes, she said—

"What fault have I committed that I should die? Why should I die without killing him who has struck me? I will not take this poison. He who has reduced me to this condition shall eat it, or, if not, I will give it to his beloved Kunda Nandini. After one of these two are dead, if necessary I also will take it."

CHAPTER XXXIII.

HIRA'S GRANDMOTHER.

" Hira's old grandmother
Walks about picking up
A basket of cowdung.
With her teeth cracking pebbles,
Eating *jak* fruit by the hundred."

IRA'S grandmother hobbled along with the help of a stick, followed by boys reciting the above unrivalled verses, clapping their hands and dancing as they went. Whether any special taunt was meant by these verses is doubtful, but the old woman became furious, and desired the boys to go to destruction, wishing that their fathers

might eat refuse (a common form of abuse). This was a daily occurrence.

Arriving at the door of Nagendra's house, the grandmother escaped from her enemies, who at sight of the fierce black moustaches of the *durwans* fled from the battlefield, one crying—

> "Bama Charn Dobé
> Goes to bed early,
> And when the thief comes he runs away."

Another—

> "Ram Sing Paré
> With a stick marches boldly,
> But at sight of a thief he flies to the tank."

A third—

> "Lal Chand Sing
> Doth briskly dance and sing,
> Is death on the food,
> But at work is no good."

The boys fled, attacked by the *durwans* with a shower of words not to be found in any dictionary.

Hira's grandmother, plodding along, arrived at the dispensary attached to Nagendra's dwelling. Perceiving the doctor, she said, "Oh, father, where is the doctor, father?"

"I am he."

"Oh, father, I am getting blind. I am twenty-eight or eighty years old; how shall I speak of my troubles? I had a son; he is dead. I had a granddaughter; she also——" Here the old woman broke down, and began to whine like a cat.

The doctor asked, "What has happened to you?"

Without answering this question, the woman began to relate the history of her life; and when, amid much crying, she had finished, the doctor again asked, "What do you want now? What has happened to you?" Again she began the unequalled story of her life; but the doctor showing much impatience, she changed it for that of Hira, of Hira's mother, and Hira's husband.

With much difficulty the doctor at last arrived at her meaning, to which all this talking and crying was quite irrelevant. The old woman desired some medicine for Hira. Her complaint, she said, was a species of lunacy. Before Hira's birth, her mother had been mad, had continued so for some time, and had died in that condition. Hira had not hitherto shown any sign of her mother's disorder; but now the old woman felt some doubts about her. Hira would now laugh, now weep, now, closing the door, she would dance. Sometimes she screamed, and sometimes became unconscious. Therefore her grandmother wanted medicine for her. After some reflection the doctor said, "Your daughter has hysteria."

"Well, doctor, is there no medicine for that disease?"

"Certainly there is: keep her very warm; take this dose of castor-oil, give it to her early to-morrow morning. Later I will come and give her another medicine."

With the bottle of castor-oil in her hand, the old woman hobbled forth. On the road she was met by a neighbour, who said, "Oh, Hira's grandmother, what have you in your hand?"

The old woman answered, "Hira has become hysterical; the doctor has given me some castor-oil for her; do you think that will be good for hysterics?"

"It may be; castor-oil is the god of all. But what has made your granddaughter so jolly lately?"

After much reflection the old woman said, "It is the fault of her age;" whereupon the neighbour prescribed a remedy, and they parted.

On arriving at home, the old woman remembered that the doctor had said Hira must be kept warm; therefore she placed a pan of fire before her granddaughter.

"Fire!" exclaimed Hira. "What is this for?"

"The doctor told me to keep you warm," replied the old woman.

CHAPTER XXXIV.

A DARK HOUSE: A DARK LIFE.

N the absence of Nagendra and Surja Mukhi from their spacious home, all was darkness therein. The clerks sat in the office, and Kunda Nandini dwelt in the inner apartments with the poor relations. But how can stars dispel the darkness of a moonless night?

In the corners hung spiders' webs; in the rooms stood dust in heaps; pigeons built their nests in the cornices and sparrows in the beams. Heaps of withered leaves lay rotting in the garden; weeds grew over the tanks; the flower-beds were hidden by jungle. There were jackals in the courtyard, and rats in the granary; mould and fungus were everywhere to be seen; musk-rats and centipedes swarmed in the rooms; bats flew about night and day. Nearly all Surja Mukhi's pet birds had been eaten by cats; their soiled feathers lay scattered around. The ducks had been killed by the jackals, the peacocks had flown into the woods; the cows had become emaciated, and no longer gave milk. Nagendra's dogs had no spirit left in them, they neither played nor barked; they were never let loose; some had died, some had gone mad, some had escaped. The horses were diseased, or had become ill from want of work; the stables were littered with stubble, grass, and feathers. The horses were sometimes fed, sometimes neglected. The grooms were never to be found in the stables. The cornice of the house was broken in places, as were the sashes, the shutters, and the railings. The matting was soaked with rain; there was dust on the painted walls. Over the bookcases were the dwellings of insects; straws from the sparrows' nests on the glass of the chandeliers.

In the house there was no mistress, and without a mistress paradise itself would be a ruin.

As in an untended garden overgrown with grass a single rose or lily will bloom, so in this house Kunda Nandini lived alone. Wherever a few joined in a meal Kunda partook of it. If any one addressed her as house-mistress, Kunda thought, "They are mocking me." If the *Dewan* sent to ask her about anything her heart beat with fear. There was a reason for this. As Nagendra did not write to Kunda, she had been accustomed to send to the *Dewan* for the letters received by him. She did not return the letters, and she lived in fear that the *Dewan* would claim them; and in fact the man no longer sent them to her, but only suffered her to read them as he held them in his hand.

The suffering felt by Surja Mukhi was endured in equal measure by Kunda Nandini. Surja Mukhi loved her husband; did not Kunda love him? In that little heart there was inexhaustible love, and because it could find no expression, like obstructed breathing it wounded her heart. From childhood, before her first marriage, Kunda had loved Nagendra; she had told no one, no one knew it. She had had no desire to obtain Nagendra, no hope of doing so; her despair she had borne in silence. To have striven for it would have been like striving to reach the moon in the sky. Now where was that moon? For what fault had Nagendra thrust her from him? Kunda revolved these thoughts in her mind night and day; night and day she wept. Well! let Nagendra not love her. It was her good fortune to love him. Why might she not even see him? Nor that only: he regarded Kunda as the root of his troubles; every one considered her so. Kunda thought, "Why should I be blamed for all this?"

In an evil moment Nagendra had married Kunda. As every one who sits under the upas-tree must die, so every one who had been touched by the shadow of this marriage was ruined.

Then again Kunda thought, " Surja Mukhi has come to this condition through me. Surja Mukhi protected me, loved me as a sister; I have made her a beggar by the roadside. Who is there more unfortunate than I? Why did I not die by the roadside? Why do I not die now? I will not die now; let him come, let me see him again. Will he not come?" Kunda had not received the news of Surja Mukhi's death, therefore she thought, "What is the use of dying now? Should Surja Mukhi return, then I will die; I will no longer be a thorn in her path."

CHAPTER XXXV.

THE RETURN.

HE work required to be done in Calcutta was finished. The deed of gift was drawn up. In it special rewards were indicated for the *Brahmachari* and the unknown Brahman. The deed would have to be registered at Haripur, therefore Nagendra went to Govindpur, taking it with him. He had instructed his brother-in-law to follow. Srish Chandra had striven to prevent his executing this deed, also to restrain him from making the journey on foot, but in vain. His efforts thus defeated, he followed by boat; and as

Kamal Mani could not endure to be parted from her husband, she and Satish simply accompanied him without asking any questions.

When Kunda saw Kamal Mani she thought that once more a star had risen in the sky. Since the flight of Surja Mukhi, Kamal's anger against Kunda had been inflexible; she had always refused to see her. But now, at the sight of Kunda's emaciated figure, Kamal's anger departed. She endeavoured to cheer her with the news that Nagendra was coming, which brought a smile to the girl's face; but at the news of Surja Mukhi's death Kunda Nandini wept.

Many fair readers will smile at this, thinking, "The cat weeps over the death of the fish." But Kunda was very stupid; that she had cause to rejoice never entered her head: this silly woman actually cried over her rival's death.

Kamal Mani not only cheered Kunda, she herself felt comforted. She had already wept much, and now she began to think, "What is the use of weeping? If I do, Srish Chandra will be miserable and Satish will cry. Weeping will not bring back

Surja Mukhi." So she gave up weeping, and became her natural self.

Kamal Mani said to Srish Chandra, "The goddess of this paradise has abandoned it; when my brother comes he will have only a bed of straw to lie upon." They resolved to put the place in order; so the coolies, the lamp cleaners, and the gardeners were set to work. Under Kamal Mani's vigorous treatment the musk-rats, bats, and mice, departed squeaking; the pigeons flew from cornice to cornice; the sparrows fled in distress. Where the windows were closed, the sparrows, taking them for open doorways, pecked at them with their beaks till they were ready to drop. The women-servants, broom in hand, were victorious everywhere. Before long the place again wore a smiling appearance, and at length Nagendra arrived.

It was evening. As a river courses swiftly when at flood, but at ebb the deep water is calm, so Nagendra's violent grief was now changed into a quiet gravity. His sorrow was not lessened, but he was no longer restless. In a quiet manner he conversed with the household, making inquiries from each one. In the presence of none of them did he mention the name of Surja Mukhi, but all were grieved at the sorrow expressed by his grave countenance. The old servants, saluting him, went aside and wept. One person only did Nagendra wound. With the long-sorrowing Kunda he did not speak.

By the orders of Nagendra the servants prepared his bed in Surja Mukhi's room. At this order Kamal Mani shook her head. At midnight, when all the household had retired, Nagendra went to Surja Mukhi's chamber, not to lie down, but to weep. Surja Mukhi's room was spacious and beautiful; it was the temple of all Nagendra's joys, therefore he had adorned it with care. The room was wide and lofty, the floor inlaid with white and black marble, the walls painted in floral designs, blue, yellow, and red. Above the flowers hovered various birds. On one side stood a costly bedstead, beautifully carved and inlaid with ivory; elsewhere, seats in variously coloured coverings, a large mirror, and other suitable furniture. Some pictures, not English, hung upon the walls. Surja

Mukhi and Nagendra together had chosen the subjects, and caused them to be painted by a native artist, who had been taught by an Englishman, and could draw well. Nagendra had framed the pictures handsomely, and hung them on the walls. One picture was taken from the Birth of Kartika: Siva, sunk in meditation, on the summit of the hill; Nandi at the door of the arbour. On the left Hembatra, finger on lip, is hushing the sounds of the garden. All is still, the bees hid among the leaves, the deer reposing. At this moment Madan (Cupid) enters to interrupt the meditation of Siva; with him comes Spring. In advance, Parvati, wreathed with flowers, has come to salute Siva. Uma's joyous face is bent in salutation, one knee resting on the earth. This is the position depicted in the painting. As she bends her head, one or two flowers escape from the wreaths fastened in her hair. In the distance Cupid, half hidden by the woods, one knee touching earth, his beauteous bow bent, is fitting to it the flower-wreathed arrow.

In another picture, Ram, returning from Lanka

with Janaki, both sitting in a jewelled chariot, is coursing through the sky. Ram has one hand on the shoulders of Janaki, with the other is pointing out the beauties of the earth below. Around the chariot many-coloured clouds, blue, red, and white, sail past in purple waves. Below, the broad blue ocean heaves its billows, shining like heaps of diamonds in the sun's rays. In the distance, opal-crowned Lanka, its rows of palaces like golden peaks in the sun's light; the opposite shore beautiful with tamal and palm trees. In the mid distance flocks of swans are flying.

Another picture represents Subhadra with Arjuna in the chariot. Countless Yadav soldiers, their flags streaming out against the gloomy sky, are running after the chariot. Subhadra herself is driving, the horses grinding the clouds with their hoofs. Subhadra, proud of her skill, is looking round towards Arjuna, biting her lower lip with her ivory teeth, her hair streaming in the chariot-created wind; two or three braids moistened with perspiration lie in a curve on her temples.

In another, Sakuntala, with the desire of seeing

Dushmanta, is pretending to take a thorn from her foot. Anasuya and Priamboda are smiling. Sakuntala, between anger and shame will not raise her face. She cannot look at Dushmanta, nor yet can she leave the spot.

In another, Prince Abhimaya, armed for battle, and, like the young lion, eager for glory, is taking leave of Uttora that he may go to the field. Uttora, saying that she will not let him go, is standing against the closed door weeping, with her hands over her eyes.

It was past twelve when Nagendra entered the room. The night was fearful. Late in the evening some rain had fallen; now the wind had risen and was blowing fiercely, the rain continuing at intervals. Wherever the shutters were not fastened they flapped to and fro with the noise of thunder-claps, the sashes rattling continuously. When Nagendra closed the door the noise was less noticeable. There was another door near the bedstead, but as the wind did not blow in that direction he left it open. Nagendra sat on the sofa, weeping bitterly. How often had he sat there with Surja Muhki; what pleasant talks they had had! Again and again Nagendra embraced that senseless seat; then raising his face he looked at the pictures so dear to Surja Mukhi. In the fitful light of the lamp the figures in the pictures seemed to be alive; in each picture Nagendra saw Surja Mukhi. He remembered that one day she expressed a wish to be decked with flowers like Uma in the picture. He had gone forth, brought in flowers from the garden, and with them decked her person. What beauty decked with jewels had ever felt the pleasure felt by Surja Mukhi at that moment? Another day she had desired to drive Nagendra's carriage in imitation of Subhadra; whereupon he had brought a small carriage drawn by ponies to the inner garden. They both got in, Surja Mukhi taking the reins; like Subhadra, she turned her face towards Nagendra, biting her lower lip and laughing. The ponies, taking advantage of her inattention, went through an open gate into the road. Then Surja Mukhi, afraid of being seen by the people, drew her *sari* over her face, and Nagendra, seeing her distress, took the reins and brought the carriage back into the garden. They went into the chamber laughing over the adventure, and Surja Mukhi shook her fist at Subhadra in the picture, saying, "You are the cause of this misfortune."

How bitterly Nagendra wept over this remembrance! Unable longer to endure his suffering he walked about; but look where he would there were signs of Surja Mukhi. On the wall where the artist had drawn twining plants she had sketched a copy of one of them; the sketch remained there still. One day during the Dol festival she had thrown a ball of red powder at her husband; she had missed her aim and struck the wall, where still the stain was visible. When the room was finished, Surja Mukhi had written in one spot—

"In the year 1910 of Vikramaditya
This room was prepared
For my Guardian Deity, my husband,
By his servant
SURJA MUKHI."

Nagendra read this inscription repeatedly. He

could not satisfy his desire to read it. Though the tears filled his eyes so that he could not see, he would not desist. As he read he perceived the light becoming dim, and found the lamp ready to expire. With a sigh he laid down; but scarcely had he done so ere the wind began to rage furiously. The lamp, void of oil, was on the point of extinction, only a faint spark like that of a firefly remained. In that dim light a remarkable circumstance occurred. Astonished by the noise of the shutters, Nagendra looked towards the door near the bed. In that open doorway, shown by the dim light, a shadowy form appeared. The shape was that of a woman; but what he saw further made his hair stand on end, he trembled from head to foot. The woman's face had the features of Surja Mukhi! Nagendra started to his feet and hastened to the figure. But the light went out, the form became invisible; with a loud cry Nagendra fell senseless to the ground.

When Nagendra recovered consciousness thick darkness filled the room. By degrees he collected his senses. As he remembered what had caused the swoon, surprise was added to surprise. He had fallen senseless on the floor, then whence came the pillow on which his head was resting? Was it a pillow? or was it the lap of some one —of Kunda Nandini?

To solve his doubt he said, "Who are you?" But the supporter of his head made no reply. Only a hot drop or two fell on his forehead, by which he understood that the person was weeping. He tried to identify the person by touch. Suddenly he became quite bewildered; he remained motionless for some moments, then with labouring breath raised his head and sat up. The rain had ceased, the clouds had disappeared, light began to peep into the room. Nagendra rose and seated himself. He perceived that the woman had also risen, and was slowly making towards the door. Then Nagendra guessed that it was not Kunda Nandini. There was not light enough to recognize any one, but something might be guessed from form and gait. Nagendra studied these for a moment, then falling at the feet of the standing figure, in troubled tones he said—

"Whether thou art a god or a human being, I am at thy feet; speak to me, or I shall die!"

What the woman said he could not understand, but no sooner had the sound of her voice entered his ear than he sprang to his feet and tried to grasp the form. But mind and body again became benumbed, and, like the creeper from the tree, he sank at the feet of the enchantress; he could not speak. Again the woman, sitting down, took his head upon her lap. When Nagendra once more recovered from stupor it was day. The birds were singing in the adjacent garden. The rays of the newly risen sun were shining into the room. Without raising his eyes Nagendra said—

"Kunda, when did you come? This whole night I have been dreaming of Surja Mukhi. In my dream I saw myself with my head on Surja Mukhi's lap. If you could be Surja Mukhi, how joyful it would be!"

The woman answered, "If it would delight you so much to see that unhappy being, then I am she."

Nagendra started up, wiped his eyes, sat holding his temples, again rubbed his eyes and gazed; then bowing his head, he said in a low voice—

"Am I demented, or is Surja Mukhi living? Is this the end of my destiny, that I should go mad?"

Then the woman, clasping his feet, wept over them, saying, "Arise, arise, my all! I have suffered so much. To-day all my sorrow is ended. I am not dead. Again I have come to serve you."

Could delusion last longer? Nagendra embraced Surja Mukhi, and laid his head upon her breast. Together they wept; but how joyous was that weeping!

CHAPTER XXXVI.

EXPLANATION.

N due time Surja Mukhi satisfied Nagendra's inquiries, saying—

"I did not die. What the *Kabiraj* said of my dying was not true. He did not know. When I had become strong through his treatment, I was extremely anxious to come to Govindpur to see you. I teased the *Brahmachari* till he consented to take me. On arriving here, we learned you were not in the place. The *Brahmachari* took me to a spot six miles from here, placed me in the house of a Brahmin to attend on his daughter, and then went in search of you: first to Calcutta, where he had an interview with Srish Chandra, from whom he heard that you were gone to Madhupur. At that place he learned that on the day we left Haro Mani's house it was burned, and Haro Mani in it. In the morning people could not recognize the body. They reasoned that as of the two people in the house one was sick and one was well, that the former could not have escaped from want of strength; therefore that Haro Mani must have escaped and the dead person must be myself. What was at first a supposition became established by report. Ram Krishna heard the report, and repeated it to you. The *Brahmachari* heard all this, and also that you had been there, had heard of my death, and had come hither. He came after you, arriving last night at Protappur. I also heard that in a day or two you were expected home. In that belief I came here the day before yesterday. It does not trouble me now to walk a few miles. As you had not come I went back, saw the *Brahmachari*, and returned yesterday, arriving at one this morning. The window being open, I entered the house and hid under the stairs without being seen. When all slept I ascended; I thought you would certainly sleep in this room. I peeped in, and saw you sitting with your head in your hands. I longed to throw myself at your feet, but I feared you would not forgive my sin against you, so I refrained. From within the window I looked, thinking, 'Now I will let him see me.' I came in, but you fell senseless, and since then I have sat with your head on my lap. I knew not that such joy was in my destiny. But, fie! you love me not; when you put your hand upon me you did not recognize me! I should have known you by your breath."

CHAPTER XXXVII.

THE SIMPLETON AND THE SERPENT.

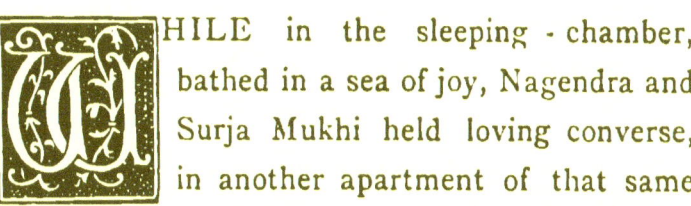HILE in the sleeping-chamber, bathed in a sea of joy, Nagendra and Surja Mukhi held loving converse, in another apartment of that same house a fatal dialogue was being held. Before relating it, it is necessary to record what occurred on the previous night. As we know, Nagendra had held no converse with Kunda Nandini on his return. In her own room, with her head on the pillow, Kunda had wept the whole night, not the easy tears of girlhood, but from a mortal wound. Whosoever in childhood has in all sincerity de-

livered the priceless treasure of her heart to any one, and has in exchange received only neglect, can imagine the piercing pain of that weeping. "Why have I preserved my life," she asked herself, "with the desire to see my husband? Now what happiness remains to be hoped for?" With the dawn sleep came, and in that sleep, for the second time, a frightful vision. The bright figure assuming the form of her mother, which she had seen four years before by her dead father's bedside, now appeared above Kunda's head; but this time it was not surrounded by a shining halo, it descended upon a dense cloud ready to fall in rain. From the midst of the thick cloud another face smiled, while every now and then flashes of lightning broke forth. Kunda perceived with alarm that the incessantly smiling face resembled that of Hira, while her mother's compassionate countenance was very grave. The mother said:

"Kunda, when I came before you did not listen, you did not come with me; now you see what trouble has befallen you." Kunda wept. The mother continued: "I told you I would come once more, and here I am. If now you are satisfied with the joy that the world can give, come with me."

"Take me with you, mother; I do not desire to stay here longer."

The mother, much pleased, repeated, "Come, then!" and vanished from sight.

Kunda woke, and, remembering her vision, desired of the gods that this time her dream might be fulfilled.

At dawn, when Hira entered the room to wait upon Kunda, she perceived that the girl was crying. Since the arrival of Kamal Mani, Hira had resumed a respectful demeanour towards Kunda, because she heard that Nagendra was returning. As though in atonement for her past behaviour, Hira became even more obedient and affectionate than formerly. Any one else would have easily penetrated this craftiness, but Kunda was unusually simple, and easily appeased. She felt no suspicion of this new affection; she imagined Hira to be sour-tempered, but not unfaithful. The woman said—

"Why do you weep, *Ma Thakurani* ?"

Kunda did not speak, but only looked at Hira, who saw that her eyes were swollen and the pillow soaked.

"What is this ? you have been crying all night. Has the Babu said anything to you ?"

"Nothing," said Kunda, sobbing with greater violence than before.

Hira's heart swam with joy at the sight of Kunda's distress. With a melancholy face she asked—

"Has the Babu had any talk with you since he came home ? I am only a servant, you need not mind telling me."

"I have had no talk with him."

"How is that, Ma ? After so many days' absence has he nothing to say to you ?"

"He has not been near me," and with these words fresh tears burst forth.

Hira was delighted. She said, smiling, "Ma, why do you weep in this way ? Many people are over head and ears in trouble, yet you cry incessantly over one sorrow. If you had as much to bear as I have, you would have destroyed yourself before this time."

Suicide! this disastrous word struck heavily on the ear of Kunda; shuddering, she sat down. During the night she had frequently contemplated this step, and these words from Hira's mouth seemed to confirm her purpose.

Hira continued: "Now hear what my troubles are. I also loved a man more than my own life. He was not my husband, but why should I hide my sin from my mistress? it is better to confess it plainly."

These shameless words did not enter Kunda's ear; in it the word "suicide" was repeating itself, as though a demon kept whispering, "Would it not be better for you to destroy yourself than to endure this misery?"

Hira continued: "He was not my husband, but I loved him better than the best husband. I knew he did not love me; he loved another sinner, a hundred times less attractive than I." At this point, Hira cast a sharp, angry glance from under her eyelids at Kunda, then went on: "Knowing this, I did not run after him, but one day we were both wicked."

Beginning thus, Hira briefly related the terrible history. She mentioned no name, neither that of Debendra nor that of Kunda. She said nothing from which it could be inferred whom she had loved, or who was beloved by him. At length, after speaking of the abuse she had received, she said—

"Now what do you suppose I did?"

"What did you do?"

"I went to a *Kabiraj*. He has all sorts of poisons by which life can be destroyed."

In low tones Kunda said, "After that?"

"I intended to kill myself. I bought some poison, but afterwards I thought, 'Why should I die for another?' so I have kept the poison in a box."

Hira brought from the corner of the room a box in which she kept the treasures received as rewards from her employers, and also what she got by less fair means. Opening it, she showed the poison to Kunda, who eyed it as a cat does cream. Then

Hira, leaving the box open as though from absence of mind, began to console Kunda. At this moment, suddenly, in the early dawn, sounds of happiness and rejoicing were heard in the household. Hira darted forth in astonishment. The ill-fated Kunda Nandini seized the opportunity to steal the poison from the box.

CHAPTER XXXVIII.

THE CATASTROPHE.

IRA could not at first understand the cause of the joyous sounds she heard. She saw in one of the large rooms all the women of the house, the boys and the girls surrounding some one and making a great noise. Of the person surrounded, Hira could see nothing but the hair, which Kousalya and the other attendants were dressing with scented oil and arranging becomingly. Of the by-standers encircling them some were laughing, some weeping, some talking, some uttering bless-

ings. The girls and boys were dancing, singing, and clapping their hands. Kamal Mani was going round directing that shells should be blown and other joyous demonstrations, laughing, crying, and even dancing.

Hira was astonished. Stepping into the throng, she stretched her neck and peeped about. What were her feelings on beholding Surja Mukhi seated on the floor, a loving smile upon her lips; submitting to be decked with all her ornaments, so long laid aside, speaking kindly to all, a little shamefaced.

Hira could not all at once believe that Surja Mukhi who had died was now amongst them smiling so pleasantly. Stammeringly she asked one of the throng of women, "Who is that?"

Kousalya heard the question, and answered, "Don't you know? The goddess of our house, and your executioner."

Kousalya had lived all this time in fear of Hira. Now in her day of triumph she vented her spleen.

The dressing being completed and all kindly

greetings exchanged, Surja Mukhi said in a low voice to Kamal Mani, "Let us go and see Kunda. She is not guilty of any fault towards me. I am not angry with her; she is now my younger sister."

Only they two went. They were long away. At last Kamal Mani came out of Kunda's room with a countenance full of fear and distress, and in great haste sent for Nagendra.

On his arrival the ladies told him he was wanted in Kunda's room. At the door he met Surja Mukhi weeping.

"What has happened?" he asked.

"Destruction! I have long known I was destined not to have a single day of happiness, else how is it that in the first moment of joy this calamity comes upon me?"

"What has happened?"

"I brought up Kunda to womanhood, and now that I have come hither with the desire to cherish her as my little sister, my desire has turned to ashes: Kunda has taken poison!"

"What do you say?"

"Do you remain with her. I will go for a doctor."

Surja Mukhi went on her errand, and Nagendra to Kunda's room alone. He found Kunda's face darkened, her eyes lustreless, her body relaxed.

CHAPTER XXXIX.

KUNDA'S TONGUE IS LOOSENED.

UNDA NANDINI was seated on the floor, her head resting against the the bed-post. At sight of Nagendra the tears came into her eyes. As he stood beside her, Kunda, like a severed branch of a twining plant, laid her head at his feet. In a stifled voice he said—

"What is this, Kunda? for what fault are you leaving me?"

Kunda had not been used to answer her husband, but now, at her last hour, her tongue was loosened. She said, "For what fault did you leave me?"

Silenced, Nagendra sat beside Kunda with bent head.

She went on: "If on coming home yesterday you had called for me, if you had once come and sat by me in this way, I had not died. I have had you but a short time, even to day my desire to see you is not satisfied. I would not have died."

At these loving, heart-piercing words, Nagendra let his head fall upon his knees, and remained speechless.

Then Kunda spoke again. To day she was eloquent, for it was her last day with her husband. She said, "Fie! do not sit thus silent; if I see not your face smiling as I die, I shall not die happy."

Surja Mukhi also had thus spoken. In death all are equal.

Struck to the heart, Nagendra said in troubled tones, "Why have you done this? Why did you not send for me?"

Kunda, with many a smile transient as a flash of lightning, said, "Think not of that; what I said, I said in the hurry of my mind. Before you came I had determined that after I had seen you I would die. I had resolved that if the *Didi* (Surja Mukhi) returned, I would leave you with her and die. I would no longer be a thorn in her path of happiness. I had determined to die, but on seeing you I was not willing."

Nagendra made no answer. To-day he was without reply to the formerly speechless Kunda Nandini. Kunda remained silent for some time; she was losing the power of speech, death was taking possession. Then Nagendra saw the death-shadowed face full of love. Its gentle light shining in her troubled face, remained stamped on Nagendra's heart to his latest day. After a rest, she said, with great difficulty—

"My thirst for speech has not been satisfied. I knew you to be a god; I never had the courage to speak, my desire was not extinguished. Death is approaching, my mouth is dry, my tongue falters, I have no more time."

She rested her head upon Nagendra, closed her eyes, and remained speechless. The doctor came but he gave her no medicine. Seeing that there was no hope, he withdrew with a sad countenance. Feeling that the last hour was come, Kunda wished to see Surja Mukhi and Kamal Mani. Both came; Kunda took the dust from their feet, they weeping loudly. Then Kunda hid her face between her husband's feet. She spoke no more, consciousness gradually departed. Her face lying on her husband's feet, the youthful Kunda Nandini's spirit departed, the blooming flower died.

Surja Mukhi, checking her sobs, looked at her dead companion-wife, and said, "May thy happy fate be mine; may I die thus, my head on my husband's feet." Then taking her weeping husband's hand, she led him away.

Afterwards, Nagendra, recovering his firmness, took Kunda to the riverside, performed the last rites, and bade farewell to the lovely form.

CHAPTER XL.

THE END.

FTER Kunda Nandini's death, people asked where she obtained the poison, and all began to suspect that it was Hira's work.

Nagendra directed that Hira should be called, but she was not to be found; since Kunda's death she had disappeared. From that time no one ever saw Hira in that part of the country; her name was no longer heard in Govindpur.

Once only, a year later, she showed herself to Debendra. The poison tree planted by Debendra had by that time borne fruit; he was seized with a malignant disease, and as he did not cease drinking, the disease became incurable. During the first year after Kunda's death, Debendra's summons came. Two or three days before his death, as he lay on his bed without power to rise, there suddenly arose a great noise at the door.

In answer to Debendra's inquiries, the servant said, "A mad woman wants to see you, sir; she will not be forbidden."

He gave orders that she should be admitted. The woman appeared. Debendra saw that she was reduced by want, but observed no sign of madness; he thought her a wretched beggar-woman. She was young, and retained the signs of former beauty, but now she was a sight indeed. Her apparel soiled, ragged, patched, and so scanty that it barely reached her knees, while her back and head remained uncovered; her hair unkempt, dishevelled, covered with dust and matted together; her body never oiled, withered-looking, covered with mud. As she approached, she cast so wild a glance on Debendra that he saw the servants were right—she was truly a mad-woman.

After gazing at him some time, she said, "Do you not know me? I am Hira."

Recognizing her, Debendra asked in astonishment, "Who has brought you to this condition?"

Hira, with a glance full of rage, biting her lip and clenching her fist, approached to strike Debendra; but restraining herself she said, "Ask again who has brought me to this condition: this is your doing. You don't know me now, but once you took your pleasure of me. You don't remember it, but one day you sang this song"—bursting forth into a love-song.

In this manner reminding him of many things, she said: "On the day you drove me out I became mad. I went to take poison. Then a thought of delight came to me; instead of taking it myself, I would cause either you or Kunda Nandini to do so. In that hope I hid my illness for a time; it comes and goes; when it was on me I stayed at home, when well I worked. Finally, having poisoned your Kunda, my trouble was soothed; but after seeing her death my illness increased. Finding that I could not hide it any longer, I left the place. Now I have no food. Who gives food to a mad woman? Since then I have begged. When well I beg; when the disease presses I stay under a tree. Hearing of your approaching death, I have come to delight myself in seeing you. I give you my blessing, that even hell may find no place for you."

Thus saying, the mad-woman uttered a loud laugh. Alarmed, Debendra moved to the other side of the bed; then Hira danced out of the house, singing the old love-song.

From that time Debendra's bed of death was full of thorns. He died delirious, uttering words of the love-song.

After his death the night-watch heard with a beating heart the familiar strain from the mad-woman in the garden.

The "Poison Tree" is finished. We trust it will yield nectar in many a house.

GLOSSARY OF HINDU WORDS.

Attar. Commonly called in England *Otto* of Roses.

Bari. The Hindu home.

Bhagirati. A river, branch of the Ganges.

Boiragi. A religious devotee.

Boisnavi. A female mendicant; a votary of Vishnu.

Boroari. A Hindu festival.

Boita khana. The sitting-room of the male members of the household, and their guests.

Bonti. A fish knife.

Bou. The wife.

Brahmachari. A student of the Vedas.

Brahman. An officiating Hindu priest.

Brahmo Somaj. The church of the Theistic sect or Brahmos.

Dada Babu. Elder brother.
Dahuk. A bird of the Crane species.
Didi. Elder sister.
Duftur Khana. Accountant's office.
Durga. A Hindu goddess.
Darwan. A doorkeeper.

Ghāt. Landing steps to a river or tank.
Ghi. Clarified butter.
Gomashta. Factor or agent; a rent-collector.
Grihini. The house-mistress.
Ganga. The river Ganges.

Joisto. The Hindu month corresponding to May—June.

Kabiraj. A Hindu physician.
Kacheri. Court-house, or Revenue-office.
Kayasta. The writer caste.
Khansamah. A Mahommedan butler.
Korta. The master of the house.

GLOSSARY OF HINDU WORDS. 317

Ma Thakurani. A title of respect to the mistress.
Mahal. A division of a house.
Malini. A flower girl.
Manji. A boatman.

Naib. A deputy, representing the Zemindar.

Pandit. A learned Brahman.
Papiya. A bird.
Puja. Hindu worship.
Puja Mahal. The division of the house devoted to worship.
Pardah. A screen or curtain.

Ryot. A tiller of the soil.

Sari. A woman's garment.
Shastras. Hindu sacred books.
Shradda. An obsequial ceremony, in which food and water are offered to deceased ancestors.
Siva. A Hindu God.
Sraban. The Hindu months corresponding to July —August.

Talao. A tank or enclosed pond.

Thakur. The Deity; sometimes applied as a title of honour to the master of the house.

Thakur Bari. The chamber occupied by the family deity.

Tulsi. A plant held sacred by the Hindus.

Zemindar. A landholder.

Zillah. A district or local division.

LIST OF Mr. T. FISHER UNWIN'S NEW BOOKS.

TARANTELLA: A Romance. By MATHILDE BLIND, Author of "Life of George Eliot," "Saint Oran." Two vols. Crown 8vo. ... ...

⁎ "Miss Mathilde Blind (author of the biography of George Eliot, and other works) has written a novel, which is to be published shortly by Mr. Unwin. It is entitled 'Tarantella,' and relates partly to the South Italian superstition as to the bite of the tarantula spider; the chief interest, however, is more of a passionate, and partly of an æsthetic (musical) kind."—*Literary Gossip, Athenæum.*

ICHABOD: A Memoir. By BERTHA THOMAS, Author of "The Violin Player," "Life of George Sand," &c. Two vols. Crown 8vo. ... ...

WILBOURNE HALL. By MARY CAUMONT, Author of "Uncle Antony's Note Book." Two vols. Crown 8vo. ... ...

CAMILLA'S GIRLHOOD. By LINDA VILLARI, Author of "On Tuscan Hills and Venetian Waters," "In Change Unchanged," &c. Two vols. Crown 8vo. ... ...

THE CHANCELLOR OF THE TYROL. A Historical Novel by HERMAN SCHMID. Translated by DOROTHEA ROBERTS. Two vols. Cr. 8vo.

THE POISON TREE: A Tale of Hindu Life in Bengal. By BANKIM CHANDRA CHATTERJEE. Translated by M. S. KNIGHT. With Preface by EDWIN ARNOLD, M.A., C.S.I. Crown 8vo   0 6 0

⁎ "The Poison Tree" is a tale of Bengal Family Life. Its author, Babu Bankim Chandra Chatterjee, is one of the most popular Indian writers of fiction, and his tales, written in Bengali, are very widely read amongst his countrymen. The story abounds in graphic scenes and incidents and sketches of character.

Mr. T. Fisher Unwin, 26, Paternoster Square.

ON TUSCAN HILLS AND VENE-
TIAN WATERS. By LINDA VILLARI, Author of "Camilla's Girlhood," "In Change Unchanged," "In the Golden Shell," &c. With Ten Illustrations by Mrs. ARTHUR LEMON. Square Imp. 16mo. ... 0 7 6

** Madam Villari's new book of Italian Life and Scenes will prove an interesting book for general readers. Visitors to Florence and Venice will find it a guide-book to the less-known and unbeaten tracks in those beautiful cities.

FAIRY TALES FROM BRENTANO.
Told in English by KATE FREILIGRATH KROEKER. Pictured by FRANK CARRUTHERS GOULD. Twenty-two Illustrations. Square Imp. 16mo. 0 5 0

** This translation of Brentano's Fairy Tales is believed to be the first done into English. Mrs. Kroeker, who recently so successfully dramatized "Alice in Wonderland," has provided an English version of one of the most popular books among the German children, and English children will find it a capital book for the Christmas season. Mr. F. C. Gould, now so well known for his illustrations in the Christmas numbers of *Truth*, illustrates the book with twenty-two vigorous pictures.

LIFE AND WORK IN BENARES and
KUMAON, 1839-77. By JAMES KENNEDY, M.A., Author of "Christianity and the Religions of India." Introduction by Sir WILLIAM MUIR, K.C.S.I., LL.D., D.C.L., Late Lieut.-Governor, N.W.P. Ten Illustrations. Crown 8vo., cloth ... 0 6 0

** This volume will contain descriptions of Life and Work in Northern India, where Mr. Kennedy laboured for nearly forty years, chiefly at Benares, and lately in the less-known hill province of Kumaon. The book will have a personal interest in connection with the author's experiences in 1857, throughout the great Mutiny; and the friends of Missions will find much that is valuable in his descriptions of Mission work—preaching, schools, orphanages, and other matters. The work also throws an interesting light on the character of the population of our Indian Empire, and gives a careful review of our rule.

THE REALITY OF FAITH. By the Rev.
NEWMAN SMYTH, D.D., Author of "Old Faiths in New Light," "The Religious Feeling," "The Orthodox Theology of To-day." Crown 8vo., cloth 0 6 0

THE WRECKERS OF LAVERNOCK.
By ANNIE JENKYNS. Crown 8vo. 0 5 0

** This story tells of the time when wreckers abounded on our Welsh coast. It relates the every-day life of a country gentleman's family of the period, and the struggles of the heroine to do her duty to God and her neighbours.

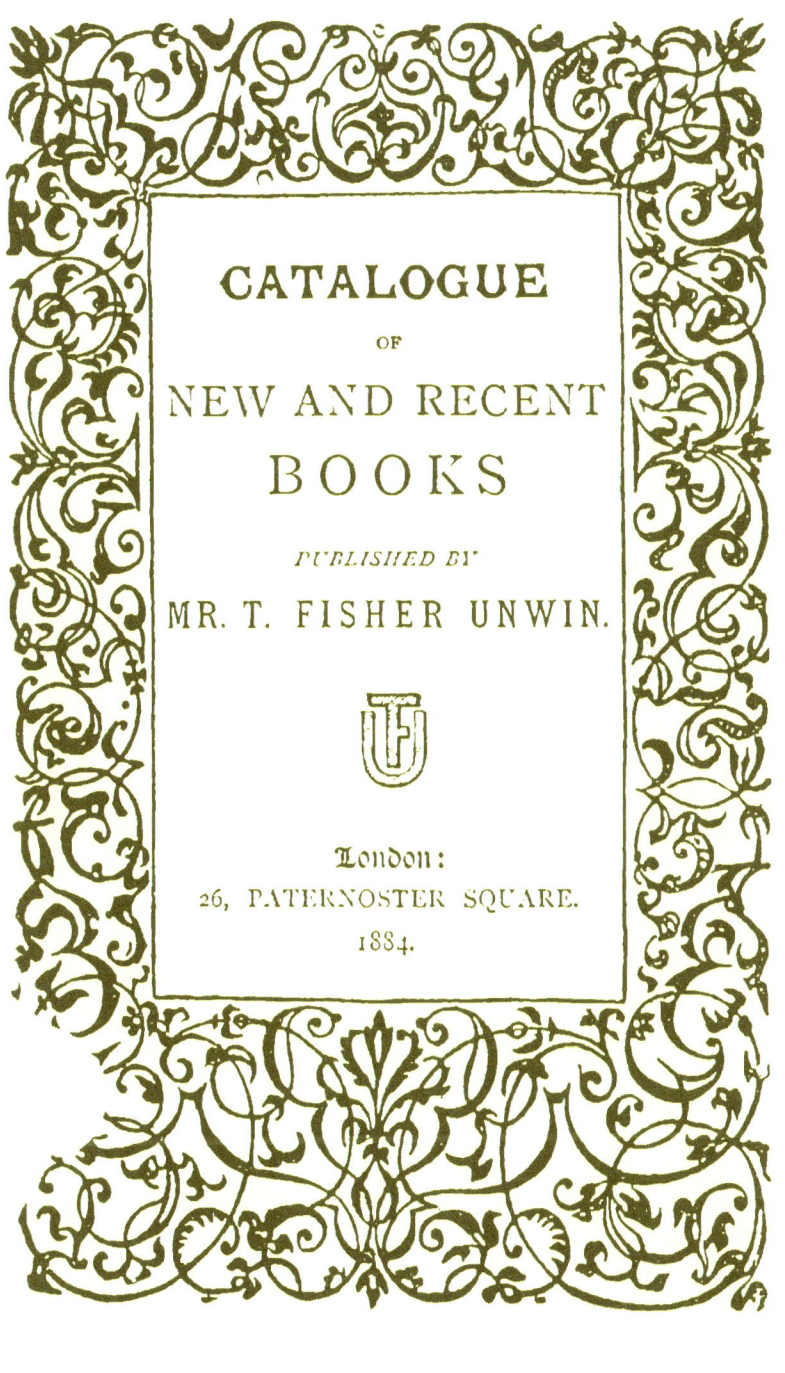

CATALOGUE
OF
NEW AND RECENT BOOKS

PUBLISHED BY

MR. T. FISHER UNWIN.

London:
26, PATERNOSTER SQUARE.
1884.

*M*R. UNWIN *takes pleasure in sending herewith a Catalogue of Books published by him.*

As each New Edition of it is issued, it will be sent post free *to Booksellers, Libraries, Book Societies, and Book Buyers generally—a register being kept for that purpose.*

Book Buyers are requested to order any Books they may require from their local Bookseller.

Should any difficulty arise, the Publisher will be happy to forward any Book, CARRIAGE FREE, *to any Country in the Postal Union, on receipt of the price marked in this list, together with full Postal Address.*

Customers wishing to present a book to a friend can send a card containing their name and a dedication or inscription to be enclosed, and it will be forwarded to the address given.

Remittances should be made by Money Order, draft on London, registered letter, or half-penny stamps.

After perusal of this Catalogue, kindly pass it on to some Book-buying friend.

CATALOGUE
OF
Mr T. FISHER UNWIN'S
PUBLICATIONS.

	£	s.	d.

EUPHORION: Studies of the Antique and the Mediæval in the Renaissance. By VERNON LEE, Author of "Ottilie," &c. In 2 vols. Demy 8vo., cloth extra 1 1 0

"The book is bold, extensive in scope, and replete with well-defined and unhackneyed ideas, clear impressions, and vigorous and persuasive modes of writing. . . . Large questions have been scrutinized in a comprehensive spirit, and are treated with both breadth and minuteness, according to the scale of the work. This will be apparent from a list of articles in the two volumes. After an introduction comes 'The Sacrifice,' 'The Italy of the Elizabethan Dramatists,' 'The Outdoor Poetry,' and 'Symmetria Prisca.' . . . 'The Portrait Art,' 'The School of Boiardo.' . . . Lastly comes the longest essay of all, 'Mediæval Love,' filling nearly one hundred pages. This is certainly a masterly performance, going over a wide field, and showing at every stage abundant discrimination."—*Athenæum*.

"It is richly suggestive, stimulating, and helpful. No student can afford to pass it by, and no library of importance should be without it. By the side of Hallam's volumes and Mr. Addington Symonds' History it will be handy as a supplement and as a kind of appendix; and as such we very cordially recommend it."—*British Quarterly Review*.

"It is a distinct advance on Vernon Lee's previous work. The impressions it records are as vividly individual as ever, the knowledge which informs it is fuller and riper. It deals with a period incomparably more interesting than the 'teacup times of hood and hoop,' through whose mazes her first work led us so pleasantly; and it has more unity and continuity than 'Belcaro.' Its title is most happily chosen, since the studies all converge upon that mystic union of the mediæval Faust with the Helen of antiquity from which the Renaissance sprang."—*Pall Mall Gazette*.

"Every page of 'Euphorion' give evidence of immense reading in Renaissance and in mediæval literature, and the author possesses the sure instinct so needful in a student of old books, which leads her to the passages where intellectual booty is to be found. . . . Deserves a most cordial welcome as a fresh and original contribution to the history of civilization and art; written in graceful and often eloquent English."—*Spectator*.

"Careful study, independent thought, and fine writing—this is a book notable and noteworthy in every respect."—*Academy*

ARMINIUS VAMBÉRY; His Life and Adventures. Written by himself. With Portrait and 14 Illustrations. Fourth and Popular Edition. Square Imperial 16mo., cloth extra 0 6 0

"A most fascinating work, full of interesting and curious experiences."—*Contemporary Review.*

"It is partly an autobiographic sketch of character, partly an account of a singularly daring and successful adventure in the exploration of a practically unknown country. In both aspects it deserves to be spoken of as a work of great interest and of considerable merit."—*Saturday Review.*

"This remarkable book is partly an autobiographical sketch of character, partly a record of a singularly bold and successful attempt to explore a country which at the time when Professor Vambéry undertook his journey was practically *terra incognita*. ... Professor Vambéry's Autobiography is *omnium consensu* a work of very great interest and merit."—*Life.*

"We can follow M. Vambéry's footsteps in Asia with pride and pleasure; we welcome every word he has to tell us about the ethnography and the languages of the East."—*Academy.*

"Professor Vambéry, of Pest, has just published a book in England that tells the story of his life; a book that forms, under every aspect, most agreeable reading. It is not only a deeply interesting account of his adventurous career, but it is also written in a light and attractive manner, so that the reader's attention does not flag for a moment."—*Die Gegenwart.*

"The character and temperament of the writer come out well in his quaint and vigorous style. ... The expressions, too, in English, of modes of thought and reflections cast in a different mould from our own gives additional piquancy to the composition, and, indeed, almost seems to bring out unexpected capacities in the language."—*Athenæum.*

"There is something in his travels which reminds us of the wanderings of Oliver Goldsmith. ... The English public will find their interest in him increased rather than diminished by this graphic account of his life and adventures."—*British Quarterly Review.*

"Has all the fascination of a lively romance. It is the confession of an uncommon man; an intensely clever, extraordinarily energetic egotist, well-informed, persuaded that he is in the right and impatient of contradiction."—*Daily Telegraph.*

"The work is written in a most captivating manner, and illustrates the qualities that should be possessed by the explorer."—*Novoe Vremya, Moscow.*

"We are glad to see a popular edition of a book, which, however it be regarded, must be pronounced unique. The writer, the adventures, and the style are all extraordinary—the last not the least of the three. It is flowing and natural—a far better style than is written by the majority of English travellers."—*St. James's Gazette.*

*** *Over Eighty other English and Foreign periodicals have reviewed this work.*

New and Recent Books.

THE AMAZON: An Art Novel. By CARL VOSMAER. With Preface by Professor GEORGE EBERS, and Frontispiece drawn specially by L. ALMA TADEMA, R.A. Crown 8vo., cloth 0 6 0

"It is a delineation of inner life by the hand of a master. It belongs to the school of Corinne, but is healthier and nobler, and in its thought and style fully equal to Madame de Stäel's famous work. We do not wonder at the European recognition of its great merits."—*British Quarterly Review.*

"Throughout the book there is a fine air of taste, reminding one a little of Longfellow's 'Hyperion.'"—*The World.*

"It is a work full of deep, suggestive thought. M. Vosmaer, in writing it, has added another testimony to his artistic greatness and depth."—*The Academy.*

"One meets with delicate and striking views about antique and modern art, about old Rome and Italy. Moreover, the plot is interesting. One cannot but feel interested in the persons. Their characters are drawn with great skill."—*Revue Suisse.*

GLADYS FANE: The Story of Two Lives. By T. WEMYSS REID. Fourth and popular edition. In 1 vol. Crown 8vo., cloth extra 0 6 0

"One of the most delightful novels it has been our pleasure to read for many a long day."—*Pictorial World.*

"'Gladys Fane' is a good and clever book, which few readers who begin it are likely to put down unfinished, and which shows considerable powers of telling a story."—*Saturday Review.*

"The author of the delightful monograph on 'Charlotte Brönte' has given us in these volumes a story as beautiful as life and as sad as death. . . . We could not 'wear in our heart's core' the man who could read aloud with unfaltering voice and undimmed eyes the last pages of this prose story, which is almost a poem, and which
'Dallies with the innocence of love
Like the old age.'"—*Standard.*

"Mr. T. Wemyss Reid, the talented editor of the *Leeds Mercury*, has in 'Gladys Fane' developed wonderful power as a writer of fiction. 'Gladys Fane' is no ordinary tale; the conventionalities of the present-day novel writer are not observed, but Mr. Reid gives us what should be the aim of all who produce light literature, something *novel.*"—*Guardian.*

"She is thoroughly original; her portrait is carefully finished; and it may safely be said that if Mr. Reid has a few more characters like this in reserve, his success as a novelist is assured. . . . It is a sound piece of work, and, above all, it is very enjoyable reading."—*Academy.*

"The beautiful and terse descriptions of scenery which we find in this story themselves suggest a genuine poetic element in Mr. Wemyss Reid. . . . We heartily welcome his success in this new field."—*Spectator.*

Mr. T. Fisher Unwin, 26, Paternoster Square.

SUMMER: From the Journal of HENRY D. THOREAU. Edited by H. G. O. BLAKE. With an Index. Map. Crown 8vo., cloth, 382 pp. ... o 7 6

This volume will contain passages selected from Thoreau's Journals, comprising his observations and reflections during the summers of many years. Some of these are descriptive, with that fine photographic accuracy which marks Thoreau's pictures of natural scenes. Other passages contain those subtle reflections on society, religion, laws, literature, which also characterize whatever Thoreau wrote, and which pique the curiosity and stimulate the minds of his readers. The book has a full index. Thoreau himself seems to have contemplated a work of this kind, for in his Journal he writes of "A book of the seasons, each page of which should be written in its own season and out-of-doors, or in its own locality, wherever it may be."

HENRY IRVING: in England and America, 1838-1884. By FREDERIC DALY. With a Vignette Portrait, specially etched from a Private Photograph taken by S. A. WALKER, by AD. LALAUZE; printed on hand-made paper by M. SALMON, of Paris. Second thousand. Crown 8vo., cloth extra ... ... o 5 o

"Mr. Frederic Daly has brought together an interesting mass of facts which will be acceptable to the admirers of the eminent actor. Mr. Daly writes with judicious moderation, and without excessive adulation, thoroughly appreciates the deservedly high position occupied by the subject of his biography."—*Athenæum*.

"Mr. Daly is a strong though by no means undiscriminating admirer of Mr. Irving. This easy and well-written narrative gives a good idea of the popular actor's career."—*Contemporary Review*.

"Conscientiously full, thoughtfully considered, and gracefully written"—*Daily Telegraph*.

"It refers succinctly to Mr. Irving's literary efforts, essays, and addresses, and concludes with a survey of Mr. Irving's personal characteristics. . . . An interesting and useful volume. . . . A portrait of Mr. Irving, etched by M. Lalauze, is admirable in execution."—*Saturday Review*.

"Written with discriminating taste."—*The World*.

"Mr. Daly sets forth his materials with a due sense of proportion, and writes in a pleasing vein."—*Daily News*.

SETTLING DAY: A Sketch from Life. By SOPHIE ARGENT. Crown 8vo., cloth ... ... o 3 6

"A charming story of real life, and one that is as true to human nature as it is true to facts."—*Congregationalist*.

"A pleasant and wholesome little novelette. . . . It is agreeably written."—*Society*.

New and Recent Books.

THE FUTURE WORK OF FREE TRADE IN ENGLISH LEGISLATION. I. Free Trade in Land. II. Financial Reform. III. Monopolies. (*The Cobden Club Prize Essay for 1883.*) By C. E. TROUP, B.A., Balliol College, Oxford. Crown 8vo., cloth 0 3 6

"Mr. Troup has written a valuable contribution to the history of the dispute between Protection and Free Trade. Though it is possible to differ from his conclusions, no one can deny the ability with which he has marshalled his facts."—*Oxford and Cambridge Undergraduates' Journal.*

"Lucid in style, and based on a thorough comprehension of economic science, the book deserves the attention of all who are interested in the questions of which it treats—questions which are likely to assume prominence in the not-distant future."—*Scotsman.*

"Leaves no doubt in the reader's mind that Mr. Troup fully earned his prize by treating the whole subject in a spirit of discrimination as well as with undoubted ability."—*Leeds Mercury.*

ORIENTAL CARPETS: How they are Made and Conveyed to Europe. With a Narrative of a Journey to the East in Search of Them. By HERBERT COXON. Illustrated with Plates and Map. Demy 8vo., cloth extra 0 3 6

"We have many new and interesting facts, put in an extremely readable form, concerning carpets and the makers and dealers in them."—*Literary World.*

"Mr. Herbert Coxon has put together on this subject a readable and interesting volume."—*Derby Mercury.*

STOPS; or, How to Punctuate. With Instructions for Correcting Proofs, &c. By PAUL ALLARDYCE. Third edition. Demy 16mo., parchment antique or cloth 0 1 0

"Is a clear and useful little book, which is written with more literary skill than is usually shown in such manuals. Mr. Allardyce will no doubt do more important work."—*Athenæum.*

"At the end Mr. Allardyce gives the useful example of how to correct a proof—an art which some of those who live by the pen never master thoroughly."—*Saturday Review.*

"We have hardly any words but those of praise to give to his very thoughtful, very dainty little book."—*Journal of Education.*

"We can conceive no more desirable present to a literary aspirant."—*Academy.*

Mr. T. Fisher Unwin, 26, Paternoster Square.

CENTENARY SERIES.

1. **JOHN WICLIF**, Patriot and Reformer: his Life and Writings. By RUDOLF BUDDENSIEG, Lic. Theol., Leipsic. Parchment covers, Antique printing 0 2 0

"Mr. Fisher Unwin has printed in delicious old text, with a frontispiece and vellum binding worthy of an old Elzevir, Mr. Rudolf Buddensieg's brief extracts from Wiclif's writings. . . . These are full of interest, and the little volume will be useful for reference."—*Graphic*.

"The matter is equal to the manner, consisting of a summary of the career of the great Reformer, drawn up by an acknowledged master of the subject, and of a judicious selection of characteristic passages from Wiclif's works."—*St. James's Gazette*.

"No better summary of the conclusions could perhaps be given than that which Dr. Buddensieg has epitomized."—*British Quarterly Review*.

"A charming book got up in the 'old-style,' bound in parchment and well printed on thick paper, containing a scholarly and appreciative account of Wiclif's life."—*Nonconformist*.

"Beautifully printed in the old-fashioned manner, and bound in imitation of vellum, this book is a thing of beauty. The specimens of Wiclif's writings are deeply interesting."—*Sword and Trowel*.

2. **THE TABLE TALK OF DR. MARTIN LUTHER**. Fcap. 12mo., Antique Paper, Parchment boards 0 2 0

This is an entirely new selection and translation by Professor Gibb, from the ever-popular *Tischreden oder Colloquia* of "The Monk that shook the world," and forms an appropriate *souvenir* of the 4th Centenary now being held throughout Christendom.

"His words are half-battles."—*Richter*.

"'The Table-talk.' The most interesting now of all the books proceeding from him."—*Carlyle*.

"Deserves the very highest praise. Great discrimination has been shown in the choice of extracts, and considerable skill in the grouping of them under appropriate heads."—*Congregationalist*.

3. **DOCTOR JOHNSON**: His Life, Works and Table Talk. By Dr. MACAULAY, Editor of *The Leisure Hour* 0 2 0

This little work will form an interesting *souvenir* of the great lexicographer, as described in its title. The first part will be a newly-written life by Dr. Macaulay, and the remaining part of the book will be short extracts illustrative of his writings and conversation.

New and Recent Books.

OUR MODERN PHILOSOPHERS: Darwin, Bain, and Spencer ; or, The Descent of Man, Mind, and Body. A Rhyme, with Reasons, Esssys, Notes, and Quotations. By "PSYCHOSIS." Crown 8vo., cloth extra, 236 pp. 0 4 6

"He is a powerful writer. . . . Many of his stanzas are happy illustrations of wit and wisdom."—*Literary World.*

"This is a clever, amusing, and instructive book."—*The Christian.*

"This work is highly creditable to the learning and industry of its author."—*Glasgow Herald.*

THE LAW AND THE PROPHETS: Being the Hulsean Lectures for 1882. By F. WATSON, M.A., Rector of Starston, and some time Fellow of St. John's College, Cambridge. Demy 8vo., cloth 0 6 0

"It is worthy of careful and critical review. . . . The book will be read with great interest by those who are interested in questions that it treats."—*British Quarterly Review.*

"Mr. Watson's lectures must be awarded unqualified praise. The lectures themselves are admirable, and nothing less can be said of the subsidiary additions, which are very valuable as confirmatory of the main arguments and theses."—*Clergyman's Magazine.*

THE CHRIST OF HISTORY. An Argument grounded on the Facts of His Life on Earth. By JOHN YOUNG, LL.D., Author of "The Life and Light of Men," "The Creator and the Creation," &c. Seventh and Popular Edition. Crown 8vo., cloth 0 3 6

OFF DUTY: Stories of a Parson on Leave. By CHARLES WRIGHT. Crown 8vo., cloth... ... 0 2 6

"So genial in its conception, and so modest in its pretentions."—*Christian Million.*

"It is a pleasant miscellany of prose and verse, with sunny gleams of humour."—*Christian Leader.*

"A playful little volume, full of cheery chat, often running away from the flats of prose into airy verse—with racy anecdote, wise suggestion, and sound good sense underlying even its fun."—*Greenock Daily Telegraph.*

"The idea of the book is well conceived and carried out. . . . The book is just the one for the sea-side or holiday resort, and only needs to be read to be thoroughly enjoyed."—*Banbury Guardian.*

Mr. T. Fisher Unwin, 26, Paternoster Square.

LIGHT IN LANDS OF DARKNESS:
A Record of Mission Work in
GREENLAND,   LABRADOR,
EGYPT,   SOUTH AMERICA,
SYRIA.   ARMENIA,
PERSIA,   ETC., ETC.

By ROBERT YOUNG, Author of "Modern Missions." With an Introduction by the RT. HON. THE EARL OF SHAFTESBURY, K.G. Illustrated. Crown 8vo., cloth extra. Second edition 0 6 0

This volume may be considered as a second series of Modern Missions (see page 11). It has been issued in response to the general demand for a completion of the record of *all* Protestant Missions throughout the world.

HALF-HOURS WITH FAMOUS AMBASSADORS.
By G. BARNETT SMITH, Author of "The Life of Gladstone," &c. Crown 8vo., cloth extra, with Steel Portrait 0 7 6

₊ Including Talleyrand, Sir R. M. Keith, Gondomar, The Chevalier D'Eon, Metternich, Harley, Alberoni, and Lord Malmesbury.

"More entertaining than many a sensational novel."—*Echo.*

The Gift Book of the Season.

THE ADVENTURES OF ROBINSON CRUSOE.
By DANIEL DEFOE. Newly Edited after the Original Editions. With Twenty Illustrations, by KAUFFMAN, printed in colours. Fcap. 4to., cloth extra 0 7 6

"This is irrefutably the edition of 'Robinson Crusoe' of the season. It is charmingly got up and illustrated. The type and printing are excellent."—*Standard.*

MOLINOS.—Golden Thoughts from "The Spiritual Guide"
of MIGUEL DE MOLINOS, the Quietist. With a Preface by J. HENRY SHORTHOUSE, Author of "John Inglesant." 136 pp., large Fcap. 8vo., cloth extra or parchment ... 0 2 6

Readers of "John Inglesant" will be glad to have the opportunity of renewing their acquaintance with this Spanish Mystic of the Seventeenth Century, through the medium of a careful selection and translation of the best things in his "Guide."

New and Recent Books.

PILGRIM SORROW. By CARMEN SYLVA (The Queen of Roumania). Translated by HELEN ZIMMERN, Author of "The Epic of Kings." With Portrait-etching by LALAUZE. Square Crown 8vo., cloth extra 0 5 0

"For this nature of literature the Queen appears to have a special gift. . . . And never has she been happier than in her *Leidens Erdengang*, which lies before us to-day. The fundamental idea of this cycle of stories is wholly symbolical. . . . The next story . . . is a piece of exquisite writing . . . It is said that for the very charming motherly figure of Patience, the Queen's own mother, the wise and good Princess of Wied, has furnished the prototype. . . . The last story of the cycles, called *A Life*, changes into an elegiac tone, and depicts an existence spent in the search of Truth. Though slightly veiled, it is impossible to ignore its autobiographic character. We have here the soul of the Queen laid bare before us."—*Literary World* (Review of the German edition).

"If to write poetry upon a throne be rare of itself, it is certainly still rarer to find Queens giving artistic form to those moments of existence that approach the mysteries of human life. Already, in her "Sappho," the German poetess, who now occupies a throne, has treated of the relationship of man to the eternal, but the antique garb somewhat veiled her purpose, while here (in "Pilgrim Sorrow") she moves amid modern as well as universal life, and is thus able to reveal the whole depth of her feeling and lament. For what has inspired her poetic phantasy is the ever-unanswered question: Wherefore and whence is sorrow in the world? The treatment is throughout symbolical. . . . It deserves to be counted among the modern monuments of our literature."—Review of the first German edition in the *Augsburger Allgemeine Zeitung, Nov.* 2, 1882.

OTTILIE: an Eighteenth Century Idyl. By VERNON LEE, Author of "Belcaro," "Prince of the Hundred Soups," &c. Square 8vo, cloth extra ... 0 3 6

"A graceful little sketch. . . . Drawn with full insight into the period described."—*Spectator*.

"Pleasantly and carefully written. . . . The author lets the reader have a glimpse of Germany in the 'Sturm und Drang' period."—*Athenæum*.

"Ottilie von Craussen is a charming character."—*Leeds Mercury*.

"A graceful little picture. . . . Charming all through."—*Academy*.

"Of exquisite literary workmanship; it is full of interest."—*Galignani's Messenger*.

"It is a prose-poem which cannot fail to exercise on most readers a refining and purifying influence."—*Scotsman*.

"To all who relish a simple, natural, and most pathetic story, admirably told, we recommend this eighteenth century idyl."—*St. James' Gazette*.

Mr. T. Fisher Unwin, 26, Paternoster Square.

THE EPIC OF KINGS. Stories retold from the Persian Poet Firdusi. By HELEN ZIMMERN, Author of "Stories in Precious Stones," "Life of Lessing," &c. With Etchings by L. ALMA TADEMA, R.A., and Prefatory Poem by E. W. GOSSE. Popular Edition, Crown 8vo., cloth extra 0 7 6

"Charming from beginning to end. . . . Miss Zimmern deserves all credit for her courage in attempting the task, and for her marvellous success in carrying it out. . . . Miss Zimmern has indeed mastered a pure simple English which fits the antiquity of her subject, and the stories are told in a manner which must provoke the envy and admiration of all who have attempted this singularly difficult style of composition."—*Saturday Review.*

"The carefulness and intelligence she displays in her selections from the 'Shāh Nāmeh,' no less than in her graceful renderings of them, are deserving of high praise. . . . Miss Zimmern's translations in this volume can be read with great pleasure. . . . A striking feature of the volume is Mr. Gosse's narrative poem, 'Firdusi in Exile,' in which is told, in charming verse, the picturesque story of the poet's exile and death."—*Athenæum.*

"Miss Zimmern has succeeded to admiration. . . . The result appears in a language at once dignified and simple, free from affectation, and at the same time sufficiently antiquated to carry us into the atmosphere of the stories themselves. . . . The choice of legends is a wise one."—*S. Lane-Poole, in The Academy.*

"Miss Zimmern has been well advised in attempting to paraphrase this work. In one volume she presents her readers with the essence and the gist of Firdusi's Epic, carrying the story down as far as the death of Rustem—that is, as far as the end of the purely poetical portion of the poet's work. She has selected well, and written the stories in a vivid style. Firdusi's stories may have a chance of becoming really popular in England."—*The Times.*

"Of Miss Zimmern's fitness for writing stories of this kind there need be no question. She has in other fields of literature shown how well she could adapt the productions of foreign writers to British tastes."—*Scotsman.*

Also an Édition de luxe, on Dutch Hand-made Paper, Super Roy. Quarto, limited to 200 copies. Artist's Proofs on Japanese Paper, signed and numbered, bound in Parchment extra 3 3 0

Later Impressions, limited to 300 copies, on English Super Roy. 4to., the Etchings on India Paper, unsigned, bound in Cloth extra 2 2 0

⁎⁎* A limited number of these editions may still be had.

New and Recent Books.

GEORGE HERBERT'S POEMS.

THE TEMPLE : Sacred Poems and Private Ejaculations. By Mr. GEORGE HERBERT. Small Crown. *New Edition*, with Introductory Essay by J. HENRY SHORTHOUSE, Author of "JOHN INGLESANT."

This is a fac-simile reprint by typography of the Original Edition of 1633. *No pains have been spared to make this an exact replica as regards paper, size, print, and binding.*

4th Edition, Sheep, imitation of Original Binding	0 5 0	
Paper boards, Old Style, uncut edges	0 5 0	
Imitation Morocco	0 6 0	

"The style of Mr. Shorthouse's dainty little preface is, we should say, nearly perfect in its kind. . . From the delicate bit of word-painting with which it opens to the closing paragraph there is one clear thought running through the whole."—*Spectator.*

"This charming reprint has a fresh value added to it by the Introductory Essay of the Author of 'John Inglesant.'"—*Academy.*

TALES OF MODERN OXFORD. By the Author of "Lays of Modern Oxford. Crown 8vo., cloth extra 0 6 0

POEMS AND HYMNS. By the Rev. G. T. COSTER, of Whitby. Fcap. 8vo., cloth extra, gilt edges 0 5 0

"The descriptive poems are very fine, especially 'The Village,' 'Early Days,' and 'The Children.' These suggest Crabbe in truthfulness of portrayal and purity of expression. The hymns are also possessed of more than average merit."—*Leeds Mercury.*

Mr. T. Fisher Unwin, 26, Paternoster Square.

MEDITATIONS & DISQUISITIONS
ON THE FIRST PSALM: On the Penitential and the Consolatory Psalms. By Sir RICHARD BAKER, Knight, Author of "The Chronicle of England," &c. &c. A verbatim reprint in modern spelling. With Introduction by Rev. A. B. GROSART, LL.D., F.S.A. Portrait and Autograph. Crown 8vo., cloth 0 6 6

"We have long known the comments of Sir Richard Baker, and we have often wondered how they escaped reprinting. . . . He turns his text over and over, and sets it in new lights, and makes it sparkle and flash in the sunlight after a manner little known among the blind critics of the midnight school. Deep experience, remarkable shrewdness, and great spirituality are combined in Sir Richard. It is hard to quote from him, for he is always good alike, and yet he has more memorable sentences than almost any other writer."—*The Sword and Trowel.*

THOMAS CARLYLE, The Man and His
Books. Illustrated by Personal Reminiscences, Table Talk, and Anecdotes of Himself and his Friends. By WM. HOWIE WYLIE. Third edition, revised and corrected. Crown 8vo., cloth extra ... 0 7 6

Reviewing the latest volumes on Carlyle, the *Spectator* of November 12, 1881, says:—"The best specimen is that by Mr. Howie Wylie, previously reviewed in these columns, a work which we know to have been read with pleasure by at least one warm and intimate friend of Carlyle, and to which, after perusing others of its kin, we return with a somewhat heightened estimate, from the point of view of the critic."

"One of the most masterly biographies—a bit of work, indeed, which it would be hard to surpass for sympathy, delicacy, liberality of view, and wealth of friendly insight."—*Contemporary Review.*

SUNSHINE AND SHADOWS: Sketches
of Thought, Philosophic and Religious. By WILLIAM BENTON CLULOW, author of "Essays of a Recluse." New and enlarged edition, with Portrait and Appendix. Crown 8vo., cloth extra... 0 5 0

"Should be a great favourite with the small class of readers who love condensed and concentrated expression, and who value a book in so far as it sets them thinking for themselves. Such readers will regard 'Sunshine and Shadows' as great spoil, as a companion in rambles, a book to be pencilled in the margin, to be taken down at odd moments as a refreshment. Readers who love Landor and Hare and Pascal will welcome Mr. Clulow's work and prize it highly."—*Bradford Observer.*

New and Recent Books.

FOOTPRINTS: Nature seen on its Human Side. By SARAH TYTLER, Author of "Papers for Thoughtful Girls," &c. With 125 Illustrations. 3rd and cheaper edition. Crown 8vo., cloth extra, coloured edges 0 3 6

"A book of real worth."—*Spectator.*

MODERN MISSIONS: Their Trials and Triumphs. By ROBERT YOUNG, Assistant Secretary to the Missions of the Free Church of Scotland. With many Illustrations, and a Mission Map. Third edition. Crown 8vo., cloth extra 0 5 0

"Tells the great story of the trials and triumphs of *Modern Missions.* It was a happy idea to endeavour to include that story, as briefly told as might be, in one small volume, so that Christian people of every Church might read within its four hundred pages the tale of what has been done in every land and by all sorts of Christians for the evangelisation of mankind. This book should certainly be placed upon the shelves of parish, congregational, and Sunday-school libraries. It is brief and comprehensive."—*Christian World.*

GERMAN LIFE AND LITERATURE. In a Series of Biographical Studies. By A. H. JAPP, LL.D. Demy 8vo., cloth 0 12 0

OPINIONS OF THE PRESS.

"This volume, as a whole, is admirable, each chapter being characterised by thoroughness, impartiality, fine critical discernment, an always manly literary ability, and, above all, a moral healthiness of tone. In fact, we are not acquainted with any English work, or, for that matter, with any Continental or American work, which we could place with so much confidence in the hands of a young student of modern German literature as the volume under review, and as special proof of our assertion we would select the essay on Goethe. . . . For this work we must express sincere gratitude to the author."—*Spectator.*

THE HUMAN VOICE AND THE CONNECTED PARTS: A Popular Guide for Speakers and Singers. By Dr. J. FARRAR. With Thirty-nine Illustrations. Crown 8vo. cloth extra. 0 3 6

"A very careful and minute exposition of vocal phenomena. Its utility is enhanced by a large number of diagrams."—*The Scotsman.*

"A work that is sure to be found of real practical value."—*British Quarterly Review.*

Mr. T. Fisher Unwin, 26, Paternoster Square.

THE ROMAN STUDENTS; or, On the Wings of the Morning. A Tale of the Renaissance. By the Author of "The Spanish Brothers," &c. With Illustrations by G. P. JACOMB HOOD. Cheaper edition. Imperial 8vo., cloth extra ... o 4 6

"A thoroughly good historical tale. From its opening scenes in sunny Venice to its close in a German village, the interest is absorbing, while the reader feels invigorated by the healthy type of Christianity displayed, as well as enriched by much knowledge concerning the ways of men who have long since passed away." —*Christian.*

"One of the best stories of the year."—*British Quarterly Review.*

AMERICAN DISHES, and How to Cook Them. From the Recipe-book of an American Lady. Crown 8vo., cloth extra ... ... o 2 6

"A smart little tome ... Fisheries and fish being at present in the ascendant, I should recommend all culinary students to turn to the section of the lady's book devoted to fish recipes and general instructions how to choose and prepare the denizens of the deep for the table ... She is great also in fish-balls ... Consult her pages likewise for baked beans, hominy, potato puffs, rye meal, squash biscuits, and minced cabbage. In soups she is strong."—G. A. S., in *Illustrated London News.*

"The author has done a really good service to the public. All who want to know what American cookery is, will possess themselves of this book, and they will be sure to meet with their reward."—*Scotsman.*

DICK'S HOLIDAYS, and What He Did with Them. A Picture Story Book of Country Life. By JAMES WESTON. Profusely Illustrated. Imperial 4to., Cheaper edition, cloth extra ... ... o 3 6

"This is precisely the book that sensible parents must often have been wanting. ... This delightful book."—*Academy.*

"A delightful collection."—*Graphic.*

"Mr. Weston has been successful in introducing a new type picture-book of the liveliest and most instructive kind."—*Manchester Guardian.*

"A new departure .... all the more acceptable on account of its originality."—*Edinburgh Daily Review.*

New and Recent Books.

I'VE BEEN A-GIPSYING: or Rambles among our Gipsies and their Children in their Tents and Vans. By GEORGE SMITH, of Coalville, Author of "Gipsy Life," "Canal Adventures by Moonlight," &c. *With an Appendix showing the Author's plans for the Compulsory Registration of Gipsy Vans, and the Education of Gipsy Children.* New and Revised and Popular Edition. 12 Illustrations 0 3 6

Her Majesty the Queen has been graciously pleased to accept, and to thank Mr. Smith for, a copy of the above work.

The Rt. Hon. Sir Stafford Northcote, M.P., thus writes to the author:—"Accept my best thanks for your book, which cannot fail to be most interesting, both on account of the subject and of the author. Your good works will indeed live after you."

"Mr. Smith's sketches of his visits to the gipsies are graphic and varied, and will, we trust, serve to excite a wider interest in the perplexing question of their amelioration, to which the author has already given yeoman's service."—*Contemporary Review*, September, 1883.

"The author of 'Gipsy Life' has so far made the characteristics and social condition of this race the study of his life, that nothing from his pen is likely to be otherwise than instructive. 'I've been a-Gipsying' will fully answer the expectations of its readers."—*The Record.*

"No imaginary picture is drawn of distant sufferers on a dark continent, for the evil, vice, wretchedness, and misery may be seen any day at our very doors."—*Daily Chronicle.*

"A rugged book by a rugged man in real earnest about his life work . . . These graphic sketches cannot fail to do good service by calling public attention to a crying evil, and so helping to hasten the day when an awakened Parliament shall wipe away this reproach from the nation."—*Christian.*

"Those who deliberately and carefully go over Mr. Smith's book will be able to see this is not exactly the sort of philanthropical work which is habitually dismissed with a careless wave of the hand."—*Modern Review.*

"The earnestness, the enthusiasm, the high moral purpose of the man everywhere shine through, dominate the book, and enforce respect alike for the author and his design."—*Christian World.*

"More interesting than any novel, and holds the reader spellbound . . . The revelations contained in this book are very startling and painful."—*Sheffield Independent.*

"Will do considerable good, and it throws a flood of light on a subject of which most men know scarcely anything."—*Christian Leader.*

"Merits a wide circulation, both on its literary merits, and the importance of its purpose."—*Liverpool Daily Post.*

Mr. T. Fisher Unwin, 26, Paternoster Square.

THE "LIVES WORTH LIVING" SERIES
OF POPULAR BIOGRAPHIES. Illustrated.
Crown 8vo., cloth extra ... ... per vol. 0 3 6

1. Leaders of Men.
2. Wise Words and Loving Deeds.
3. Master Missionaries.
4. Labour and Victory.
5. Heroic Adventure.

---

1. LEADERS OF MEN: A Book of Biographies specially written for Young Men. By H. A. PAGE, author of "Golden Lives." Crown 8vo., cloth extra, with Portraits. Fourth edition ... 0 3 6

The Prince Consort.
Commodore Goodenough.
Robert Dick.
George Moore.
Lord Lawrence.
Samuel Greg.
Andrew Reed.
John Duncan.
Dr. John Wilson.

"Mr. Page thoroughly brings out the disinterestedness and devotion to high aims which characterise the men of whom he writes He has done his work with care and good taste."—*Spectator.*

"No one knows better than Mr. Page how to put within moderate compass the outstanding features of a life that has blessed the world so as to present a striking and impressive picture. This is just the volume to enlarge the views and to ennoble the aims of young men, and to such we specially commend it."—*Literary World.*

"Here is a book which should be in the hands of every boy in the kingdom in whose mind it is desirable to implant a true ideal of life, and a just notion of the proper objects of ambition; and we may congratulate Mr. Page upon having carried out his task with all possible care and skill. 'Leaders of Men' is every way an admirable volume." —*Court Circular.*

---

2. WISE WORDS & LOVING DEEDS: A Book of Biographies for Girls. By E. CONDER GRAY. Crown 8vo., cloth extra, with Portraits. Fifth edition 0 3 6

Mary Somerville.
Lady Duff Gordon.
Sarah Martin.
Ann Taylor.
Charlotte Elliott.
Madame Feller.
Baroness Bunsen.
Amelia Sieveking.
Mary Carpenter.
Catherine Tait.

"A series of brightly-written sketches of lives of remarkable women. The subjects are well chosen and well treated."— *Saturday Review.*

New and Recent Books.

"LIVES WORTH LIVING" SERIES.

3. **MASTER MISSIONARIES**: Studies in Heroic Pioneer Work. By ALEXANDER H. JAPP, LL.D., F.R.S.E. With Portraits and Illustrations. Crown 8vo. Third edition 0 3 6

"An extremely interesting book. The reader need not be afraid of falling into beaten tracks here."—*The Guardian.*

"A collection of sketches from the practised pen of Dr. Japp, of men who have rendered good service to their race. All are graphic and very interesting."—*Nonconformist.*

"It brings before the reader a vivid conception of all the grandest chapters in pioneer effort throughout the world. There are many who must have felt the want of just such a handy book as this, and these will be grateful to Dr. Japp."—*Glasgow Mail.*

"A really excellent and readable book."—*Literary Churchman*

4. **LABOUR AND VICTORY.** By A. H. JAPP, LL.D. Memoirs of Those who Deserved Success and Won it. Third edition, Crown 8vo., cloth extra 0 3 6

Sir James Outram. | Bishop Selwyn.
Thomas Edward. | Sir Titus Salt.
Sir James Simpson. | Thos. Davidson.
William Ellis. | Friedrich Augusti.

"There must assuredly be a large number of readers to whom these stories of the lives of such men will prove very acceptable."—*Spectator.*

"We should be glad to see this volume in the hands of thousands of boys and young men."—*Leeds Mercury.*

5. **HEROIC ADVENTURE:** Chapters in Recent Exploration and Discovery. Illustrated. Third edition. Crown 8vo., cloth extra 0 3 6

⁎⁎* Containing in a popular form an account of the travels and adventures of great explorers of modern times, including Schweinfurth, Prejevalsky, Commander Markham, Vambery, Serpa Pinto, and Nordenskiöld.*

"Gives freshness to the old inexhaustible story of enterprise and discovery by selecting some of the very latest of heroes in this field."—*Daily News.*

Mr. T. Fisher Unwin, 26, Paternoster Square.

NEW AND CHEAPER EDITIONS.

GUDRUN, BEOWULF, and ROLAND.
With other Mediæval Tales. By JOHN GIBB. With 20 Illustrations. Second and cheaper edition. Crown 8vo., cloth extra 0 3 6

"This volume will be certain to charm youthful readers; and a safer or more acceptable gift-book it would be difficult to find. . . . Without some such work these precious prototypes of Anglo-Germanic romance would have remained sealed volumes for all youthful readers; they therefore owe a debt of gratitude to him who has translated, condensed, and put them into a popular prose form for their perusal."—*Academy.*

THE HOUSE BY THE WORKS.
By EDWARD GARRETT, Author of "Occupations of a Retired Life," &c., &c. With Frontispiece. Third and Cheaper edition. Crown 8vo., cloth extra ... 0 3 6

"The girls with their Quaker and Moravian training, the worthy and benevolent Mrs. Pendlebury, and society generally, rich and poor, in Perford, are depicted with skill."—*Daily News.*

"The picture he gives us here of the Enticknapp household, with its Moravian and Quaker traditions, is one nearly perfect of its kind for sobriety of taste and freedom from all sentimental exaggerations."—*Graphic.*

THE PRINCE OF THE HUNDRED SOUPS:
A Puppet Show in Narrative. Edited, with a Preface by VERNON LEE, Author of "Belcaro," "Studies of the Eighteenth Century in Italy," &c. With Four Illustrations in Sepia, by SARAH BIRCH. Cheaper edition. Square 8vo., cloth 0 3 6

"There is more humour in the volume than in half-a-dozen ordinary pantomimes."—*Spectator.*

"The preface is really more interesting than the 'Prince of the Hundred Soups,' and that—as we hope our readers will find out for themselves—is saying a good deal."—*Academy.*

"For myself, I can say that it had upon me the appetising effect of that dish in Horace which 'replaced the sated guest upon his elbow;' for though, when I took it up, I was utterly weary and dazed with the number of books I had gone through, yet I devoured it from cover to cover with a new zest."—*Truth.*

New and Recent Books.

INDUSTRIAL CURIOSITIES: Glances Here and There in the World of Labour. Written and Edited by ALEXANDER HAY JAPP, LL.D., F.R.S.E. Third edition. Crown 8vo., cloth extra   0 3 6

"Would make an excellent prize or present-book, especially for boys with a taste for miscellaneous information. Anyone, however, whose notion of a book is not limited to novels ought to be able to read it with pleasure, and can hardly do so without profit."—*Academy.*

"Dr. Japp travels through a variety of subjects, always entertaining and instructive."—*Spectator.*

"Nowadays boys are so fed upon story books and books of adventure that we welcome a book which tells them something about the facts of the world they live in."—*Graphic.*

OLD FAITHS IN NEW LIGHT. By NEWMAN SMYTH, D.D. Crown 8vo., cloth ... 0 3 6

PLANT LIFE: Popular Papers on the Phenomena of Botany. By EDWARD STEP. With 148 Illustrations drawn by the Author. Third edition. Crown 8vo., cloth extra 0 3 6

OPINIONS OF THE PRESS.

"The author has produced a little volume well suited to attract the attention and stimulate the curiosity of the student. By clothing the dry details of morphological construction with information as to the life history of plants, and by calling attention to the varied adaptations of form to function, he has followed in the wake of that numerous band of naturalists who have at once done so much to extend the bounds of botanical science, and to make it attractive to the amateur."—*Athenæum.*

"More delightful reading for the country at this season of the year authors and publishers have not provided for us."—*Pall Mall Gazette.*

"An unpretending book, whose contents cover a very great extent of botanical ground."—*Science Gossip.*

ILLUSTRATED CATALOGUE OF THE ROYAL SOCIETY OF PAINTERS IN WATER COLOURS, 1884. Comprising Seventy-five Facsimiles of Sketches by the Artists. Demy 8vo. 0 1 0

Mr. T. Fisher Unwin, 26, Paternoster Square.

NEW AND RECENT POETRY.

A MINOR POET : And other Verses. By AMY LEVY. Crown 8vo., paper board style, uncut edges 0 3 6

"A distinct advance in power on Miss Levy's former verse. ... It will be hard if her verse does not win many friends by its sympathy and tenderness."—*Cambridge Review.*

"Some of her more ambitious pieces remind one of George Eliot's poems."—*St. James's Gazette.*

"Her idea of the character of 'Xantippe' is certainly original, and several of her shorter pieces are simple, heartfelt, and harmonius."—*Whitehall Review.*

"Deserves to be singled out from the mass of every-day verse for special commendation. The book is very much above the average of such productions."—*Derby Mercury.*

MEASURED STEPS. By ERNEST RADFORD. Crown 8vo., cloth 0 4 0

"He is very happy in his 'Translations from Heine,' fully entering into the poet's humour, and deftly reproducing the half-sarcastic, half-pathetic spirit in which Heine so often wrote."—*Whitehall Review.*

"Mr. Radford is himself a poet of no mean ability, and with a good deal of Heine in his composition."—*Sheffield Independent.*

"He has imported into his deeper verse the beauty of a half-regretful subtlety and the interest of a real penetration. He can think with fineness and record his thoughts with point."—*Frederick Wedmore, in The Academy.*

POEMS AND BALLADS. By PRYCE GWYNNE. Square Crown 8vo., cloth extra ... 0 3 6

COLLEGE DAYS : Recorded in Blank Verse. Printed on Dutch hand-made paper. Fcap. 8vo., parchment 0 5 0

A RIVER HOLIDAY. The Lay of a Boating Trip. With 17 Illustrations by HARRY FURNISS. Demy 8vo. 0 1 0

"This delightful *brochure* is exquisitely illustrated."—*Society.*

New and Recent Books.

THE TREASURE BOOK OF CON-
SOLATION : For all in Sorrow or Suffering. Compiled and Edited by BENJAMIN ORME, M.A., Editor of "The Treasure Book of Devotional Reading." Crown 8vo., cloth extra, gilt top ... 0 3 6

OPINIONS OF THE PRESS.

" The book is a striking testimony to the fact that, whatever else Christianity may be, it is emphatically a power that consoles. Pain and sorrow, as mirrored in these extracts, are no accidents of human life, not evil to be endured with what firmness a man may, but something by which life is made wider, deeper, purer, and infinitely more glorious than it otherwise could have been."—*Spectator.*

BEAUTIES AND FRIGHTS, WITH
THE STORY OF BOBINETTE. By SARAH TYTLER, Author of " Papers for Thoughtful Girls," " Footprints, " &c. Illustrated by M. E. EDWARDS. Second Edition. Small 8vo., cloth extra, gilt edges 0 2 6

OPINIONS OF THE PRESS.

" Delightful sketches of girls' lives."—*Academy.*

" Miss Tytler is one of the few writers of modern times who know how to write girls' stories. It is impossible for her to be dull ; her tales are always sprightly, easy, and clever, and while she does not condescend to preach, there are admirable life-lessons to be learned in all she writes."—*Literary World.*

" Clever bits of character sketching."—*Publishers' Circular.*

THE SHIPWRECKED MARINER: A
Quarterly Maritime Magazine. Edited by W. R. BUCK, Secretary of the Shipwrecked Mariners' Society. Illustrated. Published in January, April, July, and October 0 0 6

Yearly Volumes 0 3 6

Mr. T. Fisher Unwin, 26, Paternoster Square.

VERS DE SOCIÉTÉ & PARODY, with other Essays. By H. A. PAGE, Author of "De Quincey," and "Thoreau." Crown 8vo., cloth extra 0 2 6

"We have been much interested in this amusing and instructive volume, the first half of which is devoted to "Vers de Société and Parody." ... If published alone this essay itself would have deserved to have been placed alongside of the famous Rejected Addresses."—*Literary World.*

THE ILLUSTRATED POETRY BOOK
for Young Readers. Sm. Crown 8vo., cloth extra 0 2 6

Gilt edges 0 3 0

"It is the best book of the kind which has passed through our hands for some time."—*Bookseller.*

THE WAY TO FORTUNE: A Series of Short Essays, with Illustrative Proverbs and Anecdotes from many sources. Third edition. Small 8vo., cloth extra 0 2 6

"Profusely illustrated with proverbs and anecdotes, which being throughout apt to the injunctions, are likely to act as useful memories, when the text of "The Way to Fortune" is not at hand."—*The Inquirer.*

"The author is not only a man with a large outlook upon human affairs, but with a wide and varied knowledge of English literature. Any young man—or, for that matter, any young woman—who will lay the counsels of this book to heart, cannot fail to find the way to nobility, fruitfulness, and usefulness of life, if not to fortune. We could wish nothing better for this book than to see it in the hands of all who set any value on self-help."—*Literary World.*

"This is not a big book, but it contains no fewer than fifty essays. Each is necessarily brief, and yet there is not one that does not contain a large amount of wisdom, made more effective by the help of illustrative proverbs and anecdotes. We gratefully recognise the high-toned manliness and spirituality of the skilful maker of the book. It ought to become a standard, and will make a useful present to a young man—all the more that it is certain to be read, so full is it of interest, so amusing and vivacious, as well as instructive and solid."—*The Freeman.*

MARGARET THE MOONBEAM: A Tale for the Young. By CECILIA LUSHINGTON, Author of "Over the Seas and Far Away." With Illustrations by M. E. EDWARDS. Second Edition. Small 8vo., cloth extra, gilt edges 0 2 6

SPECIMEN OF THE ILLUSTRATIONS.

Mr. T. Fisher Unwin, 26, Paternoster Square.

PRINCIPLES TO START WITH. By Isaac Watts, D.D. Introduction by Thomas Binney, D.D. Seventh Thousand. 32mo, red edges, cloth elegant, or in the new wood binding: maple, cedar, walnut, and sycamore 0 1 0

"A gem in the way of printing and binding, while the excellence of the short practical precepts offered by the writers can hardly be over-estimated."—*Rock.*

"Just the sort of book for a young man setting out in life. It can easily be carried in the waistcoat pocket, and we can conceive of no better *vade mecum*. It is seldom that we meet with so much good sense packed into so small a space."—*Congregationalist.*

THE CHILDREN'S BOUQUET OF Verse and Hymn. Gathered by Aunt Sarah and Cousin Grace. 32mo, red edges, cloth elegant, or wood: maple, cedar, walnut, or sycamore ... 0 1 0

"Love for the little ones has clearly been at work in the making of this selection; good taste as well, and a most catholic sympathy."—*Christian Leader.*

"Its little verses and hymns are selected with fine taste and appreciation of children's likings. Externally, the book is a little gem."—*Baptist.*

"One of the daintiest of dainty little books for little people. The selection of verses is admirable, containing, with some old favourites, many that will be fresh to most children."—*Christian.*

THE STARRY BLOSSOM, and OTHER STORIES. By M. Betham-Edwards, Author of "Minna's Holiday," &c. Illustrations by Miss Joanna Samworth. Small 8vo., cloth extra ... 0 1 6

DAN STAPLETON'S LAST RACE. By Mrs. Milne Rae, Author of "Morag," "Hartleigh Towers," &c. Small 8vo., cloth extra ... 0 1 6

WINMORE & CO. A Tale of the Great Bank Failure. Small 8vo., cloth extra 0 1 0

New and Recent Books.

A HANDBOOK TO
THE FERNERY AND AQUARIUM,
containing full directions how to make, stock, and maintain Ferneries and Freshwater Aquaria. By J. H. MARTIN and JAMES WESTON. With 43 Illustrations. Crown 8vo., cloth extra 0 1 0
Paper Covers... 0 0 9

⁎⁎ Issued also in two parts, paper covers, 6d. each.

"We cordially recommend it as the best little *brochure* on ferns we have yet seen. Its merits far exceed those of much larger and more pretentious works."—*Science Gossip.*

"Though what Mr. Weston has to say is comprised within fifty pages, it forms one of the best manuals on the subject we have seen."—*English Mechanic.*

"Few of the people, perhaps, who are sincere lovers of flowers and gardens, imagine the 'fern paradise' it is possible for them to make with very little trouble. To such we would commend this admirable manual. In brief compass, and without wasting words, it tells all that is necessary to be known for the general cultivation of these lovely plants."—*Literary World.*

"Those who are anxious to know the methods by which the fresh-water, the insect, the microscopical and the marine aquaria, are managed with success will do well to consult Mr. Weston's pages."—*Field Naturalist.*

ADULTERATIONS OF FOOD (How to
Detect the). By the Author of "Ferns and Ferneries." Numerous Illustrations. Crown 8vo., sewed 0 0 9

"The little work before us offers many useful hints to householders as to the detection of everyday adulteration."—*Pall Mall Gazette.*

THE BATH AND BATHING. By Dr. J.
FARRAR, F.R.C.P.E. Crown 8vo., limp cloth ... 0 0 9

"Dr. Farrar's manual is not only cheap, but it is so clear, concise, and practical that no one need fail to carry out his instructions, or in deriving wise counsel and direction from his pages."—*Literary World.*

Mr. T. Fisher Unwin, 26, Paternoster Square.

HALF-HOLIDAY HANDBOOKS:
Guides to Rambles round London. With Maps, Illustrations, and Bicycle Routes. Crown 8vo., s. d.
sewed 0 9
Cloth 1 0

I. KINGSTON - ON - THAMES AND DISTRICT.
II. ROUND REIGATE.
III. DORKING AND DISTRICT.
IV. ROUND RICHMOND.
V. GEOLOGICAL RAMBLES ROUND LONDON: A Guide to Old-World London.
VI. ROUND TUNBRIDGE WELLS.
VII. GREENWICH, BLACKHEATH, AND DISTRICT.
VIII. FROM CROYDON TO THE NORTH DOWNS.
IX. ROUND BROMLEY, KESTON, AND DISTRICT.
X. ROUND SYDENHAM & NORWOOD.
XI. WIMBLEDON, PUTNEY, AND DISTRICT, including BARNES, ROEHAMPTON, MERTON, &c.
EPPING FOREST AND DISTRICT.
HAMPSTEAD, HIGHGATE, FINCHLEY, AND DISTRICT.
GUILDFORD, GODALMING, AND DISTRICT.

The last three are in preparation.

"We could not do better than consult one of these cheap Handbooks."—*Times.*

"Those 'Half-Holiday Handbooks' are very useful. But why not 'Whole Holiday Pocket Books,' showing where to go, when to go, and how to go it? If Mr. Fisher Unwin doesn't look sharp, we shall have this series out ourselves about Whitsuntide."—*Punch.*

"Will be a boon to the weary Londoner, anxious to commune with nature."—*The Inquirer.*

"Capital guides to walks in the districts."—*Daily Chronicle.*

"A pleasant and convenient series of books for the guidance of the pedestrian."—*Literary World.*

"An idea with which we and our fellow-naturalists heartily sympathise. The series is one marked by that feeling for nature which it is so desirable to extend."—"H. W., in *Bayswater Chronicle.*

"The publishers have hit upon a good idea in their Half-Holiday Handbooks, which are likely to become popular favourites."—*Graphic.*

New and Recent Books.

"The publishers have done well in issuing these little readable manuals for the guidance of the Londoner, who, pent up all the week over his desk, or otherwise debarred from the sight of more natural objects than city sparrows, seeks in the short space granted him by the Saturday half-holiday movement, or on the feast-days of St. Lubbock, that closer acquaintance with the rural delights so necessary for his bodily and mental health. It is, of course, impossible in the short space of some seventy or eighty small pages to do more than indicate the chief attractions of localities so pleasant by nature as those above named ; but these are very fairly set forth, and being illustrated by sections of a map on the scale of nearly one and a half miles to the inch, will be found of decided utility to the pedestrian in search of an object."—*The Field.*

"Fulfil their purpose thoroughly as a tourist's companions in his rambles about districts within a short distance from London."—*Bookseller.*

"They combine the useful information of the hackneyed local guide-book with something which is rarer and more difficult to present—the fostering of a love of nature and the kindling of some enthusiasm for the objects generally passed unheeded by the run of holiday excursionists, because they have had no chance of learning how to observe, nor have tasted the delights of it. . . . The information is very closely packed, and justice is done to the lovely scenery and scientific novelties of the neighbourhood. The books are certainly cheap and well got up."—*Nonconformist.*

"The best guides of the kind we have yet seen."—*Land and Water.*

"Will be found to add much interest to a Saturday afternoon walk into the country."—*Nature.*

"Should achieve a wide popularity."—*Court Circular.*

"All models of what a gossiping guide-book should be."—*South London Press.*

GENESIS THE THIRD: History, not Fable. Being the Merchants' Lecture for March, 1883. By EDWARD WHITE. Crown 8vo., Cloth extra 0 1 0
Sewed 0 0 6

SISTER EDITH'S PROBATION. By E. CONDER GRAY, Author of "Wise Words." Small 8vo., cloth extra 0 1 0

"The three tales of which this volume is composed are not only well written, but cannot fail to strengthen those who read them, especially the young, in pure and holy living."—*Literary World.*

Mr. T. Fisher Unwin, 26, Paternoster Square.

EDUCATIONAL WORKS.
ARMY EXAMINATION SERIES.

I. GEOMETRICAL DRAWING: Containing General Hints to Candidates, Former Papers set at the Preliminary and Further Examinations, and Four Hundred Questions for Practice in Scales and General Problems. By C. H. OCTAVIUS CURTIS. Illustrated. Crown 8vo., cloth extra 0 2 6

II. A MANUAL OF FRENCH GRAMMAR. By LE COMPTE DE LA HOUSSAYE, Officier de la Légion d'Honneur, French Examiner for Military and Civil Appointments. Crown 8vo., cloth extra... 0 2 6

III. GEOGRAPHY QUESTIONS: Especially adapted for Candidates preparing for the Preliminary Examination. By R. H. ALLPRESS, M.A., Trin. Coll., Camb. Crown 8vo., cloth extra 0 2 6

EASY LESSONS IN BOTANY. By EDWARD STEP, Author of "Plant Life." With 120 Illustrations by the Author. Third Edition. Linen covers ... 0 0 7
Also in two parts, paper covers, 3d. each.

OPINIONS OF THE PRESS.

"Numerously illustrated, clearly written, with a good deal of matter packed with much dexterity into a small space."—*Science Gossip.*

"The arrangement is good; the illustrations are very numerous, there being three or four on almost every page; and the writer has done much to simplify the subject."—*School Guardian.*

"Still another primer of botany! Well, we cannot have too many, provided all are as good as this one."—*The Inquirer.*

POETICAL READER FOR THE USE OF SCHOOLS. Arranged on an entirely new principle, with Illustrations specially done for the work. In Two Parts, each 0 1 3
Or in sections separately.

OPINIONS OF THE PRESS.

"The editor of these two little volumes has managed to strike out an entirely new line for his pupils, and one which scarcely at any point crosses the beaten track. . . . To many readers besides school-children his volumes will present all the charms of novelty. The compiler has evidently a large acquaintance with the poetical literature of our country, and an excellent ear for the music of poetry. . . . The work is therefore one of exceptional interest."—*School Board Chronicle.*

New and Recent Books.

AN ENGLISH GRAMMAR FOR SCHOOLS. Adapted to the Requirements of the Revised Code. In Three Parts. Price 2d. each, or complete in one cover 0 0 6

⁂ Adopted by the London School Board.

FIRST NATURAL HISTORY READER. For Standard II. In accordance with the requirements of the Revised Code. Beautifully Illustrated. Crown 8vo., cloth 0 0 9

"Written in a simple and pleasant style."—*School Guardian.*

"The woodcuts, which are to be found on every page, will make the lessons pleasant to the scholars, and the text is wisely put in a semi-conversational form, calculated to induce intelligent reading."—*Publisher's Circular.*

THE HOUSE PURCHASER'S GUIDE: Practical Hints for all Householders. By FREDERICK SNELLING. Demy 16mo., Cloth limp 0 0 9

A CUP OF COFFEE. Illustrated. Fcap. 8vo., boards 0 1 0

"This pleasant gossiping monograph .... light and genial throughout."—*Daily Chronicle.*

THE HISTORY OF RASSELAS, Prince of Abyssinia. By SAMUEL JOHNSON, LL.D. A new edition, small crown 8vo. 0 1 0

LIST OF BOOKS ARRANGED IN ORDER OF PRICE.

	£	s.	d.
Epic of Kings. Edition de Luxe. Artists' Proofs, signed and numbered. Parchment	... 3	3	0
Etchings on India paper, unsigned. Cloth extra.	... 2	2	0
Euphorion: Studies of the Antique and the Mediæval in the Renaissance. Two vols.	... 1	1	0
German Life and Literature ...	... 0	12	0

7s. 6d.
Epic of Kings. Pop. ed.
Half-Hours with Famous Ambassadors.
Robinson Crusoe.
Summer. By Henry D. Thoreau.
Thomas Carlyle.

6s. 6d.
Meditations on First Psalm.

6s.
Amazon, The.
Arminius Vambéry.
Gladys Fane.
Law and the Prophets.
Light in Lands of Darkness.
Tales of Modern Oxford.
Temple. Imitation Morocco.

5s.
College Days.
Henry Irving.
Modern Missions.
Pilgrim Sorrow.
Poems and Hymns.
Sunshine and Shadows.
Temple, The.

4s. 6d.
Our Modern Philosophers.
Roman Students, The.

4s.
Measured Steps.

3s. 6d.
Christ of History. By Young.
Dick's Holidays.
Footprints. By Sarah Tytler.
Future Work of Free Trade.
Gudrun, Beowulf & Roland.
House by the Works.
Human Voice, The.
Industrial Curiosities.
I've been A'Gipsying.
Old Faiths in New Light.
Oriental Carpets.
Ottilie. By Vernon Lee.
Plant Life. By Edward Step.
Poems and Ballads.

3s. 6d.—continued.
Prince of the 100 Soups.
Settling Day.
Shipwrecked Mariner. Yearly Vols.
Treasure Book of Consolation.
"Lives Worth Living" Series:
  Leaders of Men.
  Wise Words and Loving Deeds.
  Master Missionaries.
  Labour and Victory.
  Heroic Adventure.

3s.
Illustrated Poetry Book. Gilt edges.

2s. 6d.
American Dishes.
Beauties and Frights.
Illustrated Poetry Book. Cloth extra.
Margaret the Moonbeam.
Molinos: Golden Thoughts.
Off Duty.
Vers de Société and Poetry.
Ways to Fortune.
Army Examination Series:
  I. Geometrical Drawing.
  II. Manual of French Grammar.
  III. Geography Questions.

2s.
Dr. Johnson.
John Wiclif.
Table Talk of Martin Luther.

1s. 6d.
Dan Stapleton's Last Race.
Starry Blossoms.

1s. 3d.
Poetical Reader. Two parts, each 1s. 3d.

1s.
Children's Bouquet.
Cup of Coffee.
Fernery and Aquarium. Cloth extra.

1s.—continued.
History of Rasselas.
Illust. Cat. of Roy. Society of Painters in Water Colours.
Principles to Start With.
River Holiday, A.
Sister Edith's Probation.
Stops. By Paul Allardyce.
Winmore and Co.
Half-Holiday Handbooks:
  I. Kingston and District.
  II. Round Reigate.
  III. Dorking and District.
  IV. Round Richmond.
  V. Geol. Rambles round London.
  VI. Round Tunbridge Wells.
  VII. Greenwich & District.
  VIII. From Croydon to North Downs.
  IX. Round Bromley and District.
  X. Round Sydenham, &c.
  XI. Wimbledon, &c.
  * Epping Forest & District.
  * Hampstead and District.
  * Guildford and District.

  * These are in preparation.

9d.
Adulteration of Food.
Bath, The, and Bathing.
Fernery & Aquarium. Paper cover.
First Natural Hist. Reader.
House Purchaser's Guide.
Half-Holiday Handbooks. Sd.:
  For List, see Books at 1s.

7d.
Early Lessons in Botany.

6d.
English Grammar.
Fernery & Aquarium. 2 pts., each 6d.
Genesis the Third. Swd.
Shipwrecked Mariner. Quarterly Parts.

LONDON: T. FISHER UNWIN, 26, PATERNOSTER SQUARE, E.C.

www.ingramcontent.com/pod-product-compliance
Lightning Source LLC
Chambersburg PA
CBHW020225240426
43672CB00006B/425